Vinologue
Montsant

Copyright © 2014 by Miquel Hudin
First edition published by Leavenworth Press, May 2014
All rights reserved.

"Vinologue" is a registered trademark.

All rights reserved. No part of this publication may be reproduced, stored in a retrieval system or transmitted in any form, or by any means, electronic, mechanical, photocopying, recording, or otherwise, without the prior written permission of the copyright owner(s).

Disclaimer: Please note that all reviews were unsolicited and not paid for by the wineries nor any public or professional institutions. Tastings were conducted by the author, editor, and a panel of professional sommeliers in Barcelona who donated their time.

While every effort has been made to ensure accuracy, the author and publisher will not be liable for any inconvenience or loss resulting from possible inaccuracies. Information such as contact details, maps, and routes may have changed and the publisher would appreciate updated information. Please write to: info@vinologue.com

Original design by Clara Juan and Roser Cerdà
Editor: Èlia Varela Serra

All photographs were taken by Miquel Hudin with the exception of pages: 87, 102, 103, 112, 113, 143, 225, 251, 255, 265 which were provided by the wineries.

Cover Photo: The cliff top village of Siurana
Author Photo by Èlia Varela Serra

ISBN: 978-0-983771-89-0
DL: B.11875-2014

Printed by Liberdúplex in Catalonia, Spain

Vinologue Montsant

A regional guide to enotourism in Catalonia including 64 producers and 225 wines

Index

General Info **11**
Introduction 13
Icons 15
Practical Information 16
History of DO Montsant Wine 22
Defining DO Montsant 25
A Rainbow of Soils 26
Vitec 27
Local Varietals 29
Local Specialties 32
Regional Events 36
Suggested Itineraries 38

Zones **43**
Cabacés, La Figuera, El Molar 44
El Masroig, Darmós, La Serra d'Almos . . 50
Els Guiamets, Capçanes, Marçà 56
Falset, Pradell de la Teixeta 62
Cornudella, Siurana, Ulldemolins 68

DO Montsant Cellars **77**
Acùstic 79
Agrícola Aubacs i Solans 83
Agrícola de La Serra d'Almos 87
Agrícola d'Ulldemolins Sant Jaume 91
Aibar 95
Alfredo Arribas 99
Amics del Gobe 103
Anguera Domènech 105
Baronia del Montsant 109
Buil & Giné 113
Cairats 115
Can Blau 117
Capafons-Ossó 121
Celler de Capçanes 125
Cara Nord 129
Cedó Anguera 131
Cingles Blaus 135
Clos Pissarra 139
Coca i Fitó 143
Comunica 147
Celler Cooperatiu Cornudella 151

DiT	155
Dos Pajaros	159
Dos Terras	161
Ediciones I-limitadas	163
Celler de l'Era	165
Escola d'Enologia Jaume Ciurana	169
L'Espectacle	171
Ètim - Cooperativa Falset Marçà	173
Ficaria Vins	179
Finca Fontanals	183
Graus de Siurana	187
Grifoll Delcara	189
Celler Els Guiamets	193
Joan d'Anguera	197
Laurona	201
Malondro	205
Mas de l'Abundància	207
Mas de la Caçadora	211
Mas d'en Canonge	215
Mas Sersal	219
Mas de les Vinyes	221
Celler El Masroig	225
Noguerals	231
Orto Vins	233
Pascona	239
Portal del Montsant	243
Ronadelles	247
Sant Antoni	253
Sant Rafel	255
Serra i Barceló	259
Serra Major	261
Siuralta	263
El Solà d'Ares	265
Terra Personas	267
Vendrell Rived	271
Venus La Universal	275
Vermunver	279
Viñas del Montsant	283
Vinyes Domènech	285
Vinyes d'en Gabriel	289

Garage Cellars 291
Coma	293
Pau & Amics	295
Ratpenat	297

Tasting Panel

Tastings were held in Barcelona during January and February 2014 at the wine bar MésDvi and wine shop Magatzem Escolà. The panel consisted of professional sommeliers that included Carlos Álvarez, Dani Garcia, Eric Vicente, Ramon Roset, Victoria Ibáñez, and Xavier Bassa as well as Miquel Hudin, Èlia Varela, Patrick Webb and Mar Galván.

Special Thanks

The authors would like to thank the following people for helping to make this book possible: Cesc Parellada for being our man in Capçanes and helping with lodging, winery introductions, and essentially making the research of this book possible, Magí Batllevell for countless visit coordination, Marc Aguiló for elusive winery information and rare bottles, the DO Montsant office for providing us with winery information, contacts and for keeping their excellent website up do date, and the Varela Serra family for a list of things that are too many to fully enumerate.

General Info

Introduction
What is this guide?

Icons

Practical Information
When to Go
Getting There & Back
Hotel Options
Traveling with Wine
Communication
Catalan Language

History

Defining DO Montsant

A Rainbow of Soils

Vitec

Local Varietals

Local Specialties

Regional Events

Itineraries

Introduction

When looking out from any point in DO Montsant the immediate element that strikes the eye is the light. The lands that comprise this Denomination of Origin in Catalonia are bright and open, old and welcoming, farmed and lived in. These are but a few of the words to describe this side of the Priorat coin.

It is the oft-repeated phrase that DO Montsant is just like DOQ Priorat which it wraps around, except cheaper. While they share the same Catalan *comarca* called Priorat, nothing could be further from the truth. DO Montsant is DO Montsant with its own unique character and style. People say they find it easier to define DOQ Priorat because the soil is 90% llicorella slate while DO Montsant has so many different soils that it would seem there isn't a common thread. But there is: history.

There are more old vines in DO Montsant than in any other other part of Priorat. But while obviously none of them pre-date the arrival and devastation of phylloxera, stumbling across wines made from the grapes of 70 or 100 year-old vines is commonplace. Then there are the families. By and large, the people making wines in DO Montsant are the same ones that have been making them for the last few centuries, or maybe even before.

The villages that dot DO Montsant are lively and singular to the point where they even have their own accents. This is in sharp contrast to DOQ Priorat where the Barcelona accent is the one most commonly heard due to the influx of outsiders in recent years. But in addition to the mannerisms, each village has its own families that managed to stay and survive unlike the 20th century abandonment found in the rugged, steep slopes at the center of the comarca.

← **Old vineyards of Joan Asens in El Masroig**

Naturally, that concept of "cheaper wines" is something that people find hard to let go and while it's true that the cooperatives (which have thrived through the last century) produce affordable entry level wines, there are countless wines of high quality and different price ranges from all the cellars. As one owner who has cellars in both DO Montsant and DOQ Priorat succinctly put it, "In Priorat I have to struggle just to make the wine. In Montsant, the wine is so much easier to make that I can make the best wine possible."

What is this guide? Flip open your favorite travel guide for Spain and within 400 or so pages, you'll find 2-3 that talk about the wines. This guide takes the opposite approach and makes the wine the destination.

It's presented as a simple, immediately approachable guide to the wine region of DO Montsant. It's full of all the wineries that visitors will encounter, information on their tastings, how to get there, and GPS coordinates.

You'll note that there are no scores for the wines because, what does a number tell you? Maybe your wine with a score of 10, or 20, or 100 is much different than someone else's, and especially than a critic who spends 30 seconds or less on a wine and ends up spitting it out. To that end, descriptive tasting notes are included to help guide you through the different wines and find those that may be your style, or those that best fit a certain situation. But these are just a starting point. Go wild, try everything and maybe find a new bottle or grape you never knew you'd love.

Winery Icons

🍷	They accept visitors on a regular basis throughout the year. You probably still need to make an appointment, so read the information section closely.
🍸	They either don't accept visits from the general public or do so in a very limited fashion, seasonally, or on a case by case basis.
🌐	The winery either has staff members or can arrange translation to English and other languages in addition to Catalan & Spanish.
👥	Larger groups of 12 or more visitors can easily be accommodated on the premises.
	A maker of "Flying Wine" in that while their wines are certified by DO Montsant, they don't own a cellar and rent facilities.
🍃	A winery with all or part of their vineyards fully certified organic and/or biodynamic. Read their profile for exact details.
♿	Those with mobility impairments should be able to visits these wineries, but call ahead to verify, especially for restrooms.
🏠	There is accommodation in the form of a "casa rural" or other rooms to rent on the premises.

Wine Icons

	A wine that represents an excellent balance of price and quality within the scope of the region.
	The Vinologue Tasting Panel personally recommend this wine based on a number of factors including its unique character and taste.

Wine Types

- 🔴 Rosé
- 🟡 White
- 🔴 Red
- 🟠 Dessert or other types

Practical Information

Spain and Catalonia have invested a great deal in being very tourist-friendly. The tourist office for the entire Priorat region is located next to the Consell Comarcal building behind the city hall on the main square in Falset. Unfortunately, they're only open in the morning except for Saturday. Additionally, they have an extensive website in multiple languages to aid visitors in planning their stay, including a calendar of events and a list of tour agencies.
www.turismepriorat.org

Guides For those who wish to have a guided trip to the region, there are many tour operators based in Barcelona who offer a "Priorat package". While convenient, the best experience for visitors will be had through those with intimate knowledge of the region, such as with the author of this guide, Miquel Hudin, who offers personal tours to both DO Montsant and neighboring DOQ Priorat.

The tourism office in Priorat can help you to find a guide as well, although they'll most likely just put you in contact with Rachel Ritchie who has lived in Priorat for years and is not only fluent in Catalan and Spanish but also speaks countless other languages.

Alternatively, if you want to experience more of the nature of Priorat combining hiking with winery visits, contact El Brogit. They offer one or multiple-day package trips that take visitors through the historic trails of the Priorat with stopovers at local wineries.
www.hudin.com, www.rachelritchie.com, www.elbrogit.com

When to Go

The general rule of thumb for any time of the year is to call beforehand to make sure it's a good time for the cellar as many are small without a specific person assigned to visits. Some prefer visits during weekends as they live elsewhere or are in the fields during the week, while others will prefer weekdays.

While by definition wineries run year-round, there are indeed times that are more ideal than others. December, January and February are typically the worst as it is incredibly cold and most people go out as little as possible.

March through May is a much better time. While there may be rain, the weather is warmer and life comes back to the cellars and vineyards, with lots of flowers and trees blossoming. The best time, if you're able to deal with a pinch of heat is June, July, and early September. August can be decent, but people are often at the beach as the temperatures are incredibly hot.

Harvest (late September through October) can be the best and the worst time to visit. Some wineries don't take visitors during this time as they're incredibly busy, working 16-hour days, every day of the week. Others are more than happy to have visitors as it allows people to see the winery in full swing, and a handful of them even offer harvest-related activities. November is quite nice, but many people take off a week or two given how intense the harvest is.

Getting There & Back

Plane Most people arriving internationally will land in Barcelona's El Prat airport. From there, a local train or the Aerobus take people to the Barcelona city center. As an alternative, there is the Reus airport just 25km away from Priorat. The primary carrier is the budget airline, Ryanair with a connecting bus once an hour to the center of Reus.

Car Rental Rental cars are plentiful in this tourist-friendly part of the world, although you need to keep in mind that the alcohol limit for driving is 0.05%. There are also many, many police checkpoints as well as portable radar speed detectors during the high season and holiday weekends, so make sure to designate a driver and watch the speed. Cars are also not cheap to rent in the high season and will put a huge dent in your budget. But, to visit most of the wineries on your own, they're completely necessary. Just remember that there are only two gas stations in the region: Falset and Cornudella de Montsant.

While it's possible to hire a car in Barcelona, it's also possible in Reus (both in the center and at the airport) for those wishing to avoid the drive in and out of Catalonia's sprawling capital city. Make sure to reserve online ahead of time to save money and ensure you get a car.

Train & Bus Amazingly, despite the small size and remoteness to the villages, it is possible to visit Priorat without a car. It isn't easy though. The best arrival point from Barcelona is the Marçà-Falset station although Capçanes is very convenient as well. From Marçà-Falset a shuttle bus runs the route between the station, Marçà, and Falset. At just 2.5km from town, one can also walk or ride a bicycle.

To get to the wineries, there are several local bus routes that run through most of the main villages in the comarca. The schedules aren't terribly frequent, but they can work

to have a few decent visits. Consult the main bus website, walk up to the main depot on the north side of Falset, or ask at the tourism office.
www.renfe.com, www20.gencat.cat/portal/site/mobilitat

Alternatively, you can rent a bicycle in Barcelona's wealth of bike rental shops and take it with you in the train. However, bear in mind that while distances in Priorat are short, the roads are twisty and often steep once you leave Falset.

Hotel Options

There are several hotel options in Priorat worthy to note. The largest and most classic is Hostal Sport in Falset which has both a hotel and restaurant. There are smaller hotels around the villages that are noted in the village sections.

Beyond hotels though, the most common lodging option are the "cases rurals". These are old homes in rural areas that have been renovated to accept guests with one of the most well-known being Mas Figueres in Marçà.

Traveling with Wine

More than likely, when visiting wineries you will buy a bottle... or maybe 12 of something you like. With shipping costs for wine costing more than the wine itself, how do you take it home with you? One trick is to wrap the bottles in the dirty clothes in your suitcase. It is indeed possible that a bottle could still break, but keep in mind that bottles are quite strong. The key is to make sure that they don't have direct contact with one another, but read up:
www.enotourist.net/traveling-with-wine/

Winery Communication

All methods to contact wineries are listed in their profiles. Most have functioning email accounts and some (not many) are fantastic with responding while others make you feel like your message fell in to a digital black hole. If you don't hear a response a day or two after sending a message, try the phone number listed.

Telephone numbers in Spain are comprised of nine digits and the international country code is +34. Fixed lines start with a 9 and more specifically in Priorat, they start with 977. Mobile phones typically start with a 6 and will be more expensive to call from a land line.

Also very popular in Spain is WhatsApp if you're familiar with it and people respond more rapidly in general.

Catalan Language

Catalonia wasn't always a part of Spain. It was its own kingdom for centuries and then a joint, but equal kingdom with neighboring Aragón for several more. But, on September 11, 1714 Barcelona fell in the War of Succession and for the last 300 years, it has been, much to the chagrin of the Catalans, under the Spanish Crown. There have been attempts to establish an independent Catalonia throughout this time, but none have managed to succeed.

As Catalonia is administratively part of Spain, first-time visitors are often under the impression that Catalan is a dialect of Spanish. While Latin-based, it's a Romance language in its own right and is as related to Spanish (or Castilian, as it's called in Spain) as Spanish is to Italian or French. Want further proof? Take the simple example of "a sandwich with ham and cheese". In Castilian this is, "un bocadillo con jamón y queso". In Catalan, it's "un entrepà amb pernil i formatge".

Catalan is the only official language of Andorra and a co-official language with Castilian in the Spanish autonomous communities of Catalonia, the Balearic Islands, and Valencia. It is also spoken in the historic northern Catalan region of Roussillon in southern France. Since education in Catalonia is in both Castilian and Catalan, most everyone in the region is completely bilingual and you will have no problem communicating in Castilian with the Catalan winemakers listed in this guide. But, as you will see, towns, streets, and grapes are all written with Catalan spellings.

Note that Catalan has two main dialects, Eastern and Western, with differences in pronunciation. The Priorat dialect is the Western variant and differs a bit from the one spoken in Barcelona.

For those wishing to delve further in to the language, you will be met with open arms by the Catalans, who appreciate outsider interest in their language as it is looked upon with annoyance by Castilian speakers. There are books you can buy such as "Teach Yourself Catalan" by Alan Yates and Anna Poch or "Catalan: A Comprehensive Grammar" by Max Wheeler.

Online resources:
www.parla.cat
www.wikipedia.org/wiki/Catalan_grammar
en.wikivoyage.org/wiki/Catalan_phrasebook

To learn more:
en.wikipedia.org/wiki/Catalan_language
en.wikipedia.org/wiki/History_of_the_Catalan_language

History of DO Montsant

First Period: Antiquity – 1163
The initial history of wine in Priorat can be dated back to Roman times. The capital of this region was Tarragona which was a day's journey to the east of Priorat. While the Romans (and the Greeks before them) had been producing wine in Catalonia, there is only limited evidence that wine was produced in the Priorat comarca such as amphorae found in the village of Marçà which are assumed to have been used to make wine. There are many ruins scattered about the region that can be dated back to the Roman period and records from noted Roman historians such as Pliny the Elder that speak of the wines from Tarraco, the Roman name for Tarragona.

In the 8th century, the region fell under Moorish, Muslim control which put a stop to any winemaking in the region. It would remain under their control until the 12th century only to be completely "re-conquered" with the final taking of the high mountain village of Siurana in 1153, marking the end of Moorish control in Catalonia.

Second Period: 1163 – 1835
It's the later 12th century where things start to get interesting again in terms of wine. In 1163, Alfons el Cast founded the "Cartoixa de Santa Maria d'Escaladei" establishing the first Carthusian monastery in the Iberian Peninsula. The location in a secluded valley by the Montsant bluff was where a shepherd had a vision of angels climbing a staircase to heaven, thus the name, "scala dei" or "stairs to god".

Naturally, where Christian monks go, the wine shall follow. The lands that were established around the monastery became the priory or, in Catalan, "priorat" and all the villages in the region became heavily integrated in to the monks' winemaking. Throughout the 13th to the early 17th century, the power and wealth of this monastery grew immense-

ly as they gained control of more lands and became a feudal lord of the region. They also sent out monks to many other regions in Iberia to establish more monasteries.
All was not well though and the people of the region grew weary of the heavy taxes and tributes they had to pay to the monastic order. The monastery's lands were initially stripped in 1820, but returned three years later to only then see them completely and finally stripped by the 1835 Ecclesiastical Confiscations of Mendizábal. This Spain-wide privatization of church lands that were largely unused saw the end of many centuries-old orders.

The local residents in Priorat, tools in hand, took a great deal of pleasure in sacking and destroying the monastery. The ruined state it sits in today is not due to centuries of sun and rain, but the peasantry taking out their aggression on what they saw to be an oppressive landlord.

Third Period: 1835 – 1910
Winemaking continued on a smaller scale after the demise of the monastery and in 1893, the phylloxera plague found its way south from France. By the end of the 19th century, it had decimated every single vine in the region.

Most people finally gave up on the harsh environment in the center of the Priorat comarca, threw in the proverbial towel, and left for cities like Tarragona or Barcelona. Those who stayed were in the flatter, outlying villages of the comarca and while they had to replant their vines, recovery was faster as in addition to grapes, they also grew olives, nuts, and other crops.

Fourth Period: 1910 – 2001
Those who remained found safety in numbers though and formed cooperatives to make their wines together to share facilities and risk as well as control the quality which until that point had been up and down due to most winemakers being home winemakers.

Eleven large cooperatives started during this period in all of the main villages including: Cabacés, La Figuera, El Molar, El Masroig, La Serra d'Almos, Els Guiamets, Capçanes, Marçà, Falset, Cornudella de Montsant, and Ulldemolins. While Marçà and Falset merged in 1999 and Els Guiamets was sold to Cellers Unió in 2013, all of these cooperatives are still in operation today although Cabacés doesn't make wine anymore. In 1976 DO Tarragona was officially created and marked a change for the cooperatives who had been dealing almost exclusively in bulk wine production, but made the shift to bottled wines and the start of higher quality wines.

Fifth Period: 2001 - ?
The biggest change for the region came in 2001 with the creation of DO Montsant that was born of the DO Tarragona subzone of Falset and geographically wraps around the DOQ Priorat which was founded much earlier in 1954 to encompass the villages that had historically been tied to the priory. Wines started being released as DO Montsant in 2002 and there has been a marked increase in quality and demand since this change.

Another change has been that the numbers of associates at the cooperatives have been dwindling. While there has been natural attrition over the years due to viticulture being hard work and younger generations not wanting to continue, it's also the case that many previous members of the cooperatives have started making their own DO Montsant wines. This DO started with 28 cellars in 2001, but now officially lays claim to 59.

The 2008 Global Financial Crisis did take its toll on the cellars (such as the 70% drop in exports) as it did in DOQ Priorat but it wasn't nearly as severe. Given that these cellars are familial cellars and old ones at that, they have had much less debt and were able to weather bad times, just like they have been for generations.

Defining DO Montsant

With its foundations dating back to the 17th century, Spain established a formal Denominación de Origen (or DO) structure for wine in the 1920s, although it was revised several times throughout the 20th century to arrive in 1996 at the system in place today. There are currently 12 official DO certifications issued within the territory of Catalonia.

The DO, at its core is a system of quality control. It exists in a similar form in both France and Italy. Given that terms such as "artisanal" carry little official weight, the DO acts as a regulation body to ensure that wine as well as food meets a set of standards set forth by semi-autonomous governing bodies. They inspect wineries to ensure that compliance is met and they issue labels for winemakers to affix to their bottles to denote certification. They control the types of grapes that can be used, the geographic area where the grapes can be sourced from as well as how the wines must be aged and stored.

For some this may come as a foreign concept. For example there is no equivalent body in the US. Even though the American Viticultural Area, or AVA designation of regions exists there, it isn't in any way comparable to the regulation system of the DO and has no certification element.

The wines in this guide are certified by the DO Montsant which was established in 2001 and named after the impressive mountain range that in Catalan means, "holy mountain". The name, "Montsant" is protected and all wines that are certified with this label must be grown and produced within the boundaries of the DO region. Wines must be no more than 15% in alcohol unless they're Grenache which can be up to 20%.

There are many, many more regulations that are quite stringent up until the wine is tasted by a committee of experts and officially released as a "certified" wine.

A Rainbow of Soils

While DO Montsant's sibling next door, DOQ Priorat has mostly one type of soil, llicorella slate, DO Montsant has a great wealth of soil types. While this can make it more intricate to define that "thing" that is the backbone of character in DO Montsant, it also offers up a great variety of diversity and many cellars wisely capitalize on that by creating single varietal bottlings to thoroughly show where the wine comes from and the difference that the soil makes. The DO has even started to award a seal to wineries whose single varietal wines score highly with their tasting panel.

Compact These are sedimentary, calcareous soils with a high clay content that are often found near rivers, especially in the southern areas.

Gravel Found mostly near Falset and comes from the erosion of larger stones. Poor in both organic matter and holding water, which means they make the vines suffer and produce great grapes.

Stony Formed by the llicorella slate that is typical of the area. Also poor in organic matter and water holding ability, they'll often have a good amount of red clay to them.

Vitec

Technologically, we've come a long way in wine production since we just tossed grapes in a vat, waited for them to ferment and poured out the wondrous red drink we all know as wine. Maybe we went a little too far with technology and there are some winemakers around the world who are returning to older methods of production, but even still, they're doing it with the help of places such as Vitec.

Based in Falset just across the road from the enology school, Vitec is a vital part to modern wine production. While there are similar facilities such as those at Incavi in Penèdes, the southern winemakers wanted to have direct access to a facility to analyze their wines and fine tune the entire process. Vitec was the answer.

Construction started in 2005 and opened in 2009 just after everything blew up in the Global Financial Crisis. While the building was finished and the equipment was installed, their government funding ran dry and they had no way to run the place day to day. Necessity being the mother of invention, they worked to market themselves to the wineries by offering various packages to analyze the wines at many different price levels. This brought in a lot of smaller wine-

makers who previously hadn't made use of such facilities. This in turn has improved quality for everyone and made the Catalan wines achieve the high levels that they've been reaching for the last few years.

The services they offer are dizzying and a tour by director, Sergi de Lamo of the various laboratories shows no end of ongoing projects. In one room they've chopped off the tops of bottles with the corks in to analyze exactly how much oxygen passes through the cork. In another room sits a device that looks like it's been sent back from the 22nd century and is used to remove alcohol from wine. In another room and out in the back are what look like endless beer kegs, but these are actually microvinifications that they run for winemakers to see how small amounts of wine will turn out under various conditions in order to see which direction will be best for the rest of their wine. Very cool stuff.

It's not just all laboratory work though as there's a very clean, quiet white room with many small tables around it for tasting. All of the big names in wine reviewing come here to taste through the wines from DOQ Priorat and DO Montsant as it offers a tranquil, controlled environment to focus on the wines. They even have partitions that can be inserted to block out as much of the world around them as possible.

While they don't offer tours, Vitec has become a key part to wine production and you can taste it with every bottle that comes out of the region.

Local Varietals

As several of the grapes that the wineries in DO Montsant use are actually native to the region, they have different names than those used in English—which are often just derived from the French names. Below is a chart comparing the names in a variety of languages for easy reference.

English	Catalan /Castilian
Carignan	Samsó, Carinyena / Cariñena, Mazuela
Grenache	Garnatxa, Lledoner / Garnacha
Hairy Grenache	Garnatxa Peluda / Garnacha Peluda
Macabeu	Macabeu / Macabeo, Viura
Piquepoul	Picapoll / Picapoll
Tempranillo	Ull de Llebre /Tempranillo
Muscat	Moscatell / Moscatel

There are officially 15 varietals allowed for wine production in DO Montsant with five of those being preferred and seen as best suited for the region. A wine must list a maximum of five varietals on the label unless one comprises less than 5% of the finished blend.

White Grapes
Chardonnay, White Grenache, Macabeu, Muscat Blanc à Petits Grains, Xarel·lo, Parellada

Red Grapes
Red Grenache, Carignan, Hairy Grenache, Cabernet Sauvignon, Mourvèdre, Tempranillo, Red Piquepoul, Merlot, Syrah

Carignan

Known in Spanish as Cariñena and in Catalan as either Carinyena or Samsó, this grape is thought to originally be from the Cariñena area in the Aragón region of Spain that's immediately west of Catalonia. It has been grown in Catalonia for as long anyone can remember and is actually rarely found in Cariñena these days. It's in France where it gained a rather horrible reputation as a grape given that in the Languedoc-Roussillon region they planted it to over-produce. The results were rather unfortunate, sharp wines and many of these vines have since been torn out.

In DO Montsant, there is a great wealth of old growth Carignan vineyards and they produce wonderfully mature and subtle wines that can age for years. It still requires a great deal of skill to produce these wines and the best vines are usually found on the old, steep slopes that are plentiful about the region.

The name in Catalan of Samsó can be confusing though, as in French there is a different grape called Cinsault which sounds nearly identical. The Catalans have used Samsó primarily to avoid confusion with the DO Cariñena region, as the term Cariñena/Carinyena is protected by that DO. Several wineries in DO Montsant don't care for the Samsó name which they feel is artificial and simply write the grape as the intentionally misspelled "Caranyena".

Grenache

Known as Garnacha in Spanish and Garnatxa or Lledoner in Catalan, this grape is heavily planted across the region. They make heavy use of both the red and white variants which have established themselves as workhorse grapes for Catalonia as a whole. Despite the French name that is used in English, it is very much a Catalan grape. While it gained popularity in neighboring Aragón, it grows fantastically well in DO Montsant.

Full bodied and throaty, yet elegant, as a red it is typically blended with Carignan, although a good number of single varietal bottles of Red Grenache are easy to find. As a white grape it is also robust and loves to toss out all manner of minerality that allows it to be blended quite well with Macabeu.

as such is blended with "regular" Grenache grapes or others with more depth to them. That said, Teixar from Vinyes Domènech is a 100% single varietal bottling that's fanastic.

Macabeu

This white grape is apparently originally from the Valencia region, but has been widely planted in Catalonia as well as in Rioja where it acquired the less commonly used name of Viura. It is never found as a single varietal wine in DO Montsant. Macabeu is quite popular to use in a blend with White Grenache to create a very nicely balanced bottle.

Singularly, it typically has floral aspects to the nose and is rather light in the body.

Hairy Grenache

It's often the case that Garnatxa Peluda (Garnacha Peluda) gets lumped in to just being yet another type of Grenache. While definitely related to the standard Grenache, it is a distinctly different grape. The name which means, "Hairy Grenache" is due to the downy undersides of leaves that evolved to protect the vine from transpiration in the heat, conserve moisture and reduce stress. The grapes also have considerably thicker skins and it is a rather hardy grape, particularly resistant to high winds. It can have a wonderful, massive bouquet with dark aspects such as anise and fennel. But it generally has lower alcohol and very little body and

Local Specialties

Cóc/Coca de Recapte
There are endless variations of coca in Catalonia, called cóc in the Tarragona area, which basically means flatbread. Many of them are sweet, but the vegetable ones are the most interesting. Some may find them similar to pizza, but their origin is older and didn't use to have a tomato base. They're typically made with seasonal toppings and not much else other than bread, but these days it's common to find llonganissa sausage or tuna versions. For Saint Blaise on February 3rd, several meter long coques are paraded around the streets of Falset and then eaten afterwards.

Menjablanc
Menjablanc or menjarblanc (literally, "white meal") is an ancient, simple custard dessert made primarily from almond milk, a touch of lemon peel, sugar and cinnamon. Authentic versions are topped with hazelnuts. Local legend says it became popularized by a monk in Scala Dei.

Clotxa
In a similar way as coca de recapte, clotxa ('cloacha') was traditionally eaten while working in the fields. It is a round loaf of bread that has been hollowed out and filled with sardines or herrings and grilled vegetables.

Olives
Wine gets all the glory, but the olives are glorious. They can be found in a multitude of locations. Most bars and restaurants will have them as a snack and most any shop with a few groceries will sell them.

Olive oil
All the olive oil produced in the Priorat comarca falls under the protected denomination of Siurana that certifies its quality. It is of extremely high quality, very aromatic, and simply delicious. Almost all of it made with Arbequina olives, although some producers like Miró Cubells make oils with other local varieties such as rojals. His Cavaloca oil has won numerous awards and can be found at the family shop in Escaladei next to Cellers de Scala Dei. They also do oil tastings at the shop and offer visits of their oil press in Cabacés. And check out "Oli del raig" which is a first press olive oil made only at the very start of the olive harvest.

Truita amb Suc
Truita is the Catalan name for an omelet, called "tortilla" in Spanish (not to be confused with the flour or corn tortilla from Mexico). This specific variation on the dish is "juicy" in that some sauce is added to the truita to turn it into a main dish. There are many variations on this omelet, some with spinach, others with beans, but they're all delicious. You'll often find them at local festivals and Ulldemolins even puts on an event in March devoted entirely to it.

Vermut
This is an old tradition that has seen a resurgence in the rest of Catalonia lately, but never went out of style in southern regions such as Priorat. To put it succinctly, it's a pre-meal snack paired with a Vermut, a local wine-based drink that has a bitter component to it that whets the appetite. If this sounds familiar to Vermouth, it's because it is. The Catalan take on it sees people eating a couple of olives, chips, and other small bites along with a small glass of the drink. You haven't really experienced Priorat unless you've made sure to fit a Vermut in to your Sunday. A number of the wineries in the area make a Vermut wine and it's definitely worth a taste.

La Quinta Essència dels Llops/BCN Gin
There used to be a great many distilleries in this region, but they nearly disappeared until Philippe Geerarset and his wife Brigitte came to the region from Belgium and worked tirelessly to create a small, craft still in their home to make the traditional "aiguardent" from the pomace of Clos Mogador. The result is a wonderfully elegant alcohol with various herbal notes that are from Philippe's proprietary recipe. They've also branched out with another herbal liquor as well as an excellent craft Gin made from the alcohol they distill called BCN Gin. It's infused with herbs from the Priorat area and has a fantastic array of botanical aromas.

Avellanes
These are not specifically from Priorat, but the hazelnuts grown in the Tarragona area are famous all over Spain and like no other hazelnut you've tried. The same hard growing conditions that make great wines also make great nuts and these are rich, buttery in flavor, and insanely addictive.

Regional Events

May is typically the busiest month for wine-related events in all of Priorat, although there are a few others throughout the year:

Priorat Wine Fair in Falset
The first weekend in May, Falset fills up with people for the largest wine fair of the Priorat region. Wineries from both DOQ Priorat and DO Montsant offer tastings at the fair but also at many parallel events around town such as the Vide-Nit at Mas Figueres. It presents a fantastic opportunity for visitors to taste everything from the region in a very festive environment. If you're planning to go, book your accommodation well ahead as 15,000+ people descend on the region for this event.
www.firadelvi.org

Festes Majors
Every village in Priorat celebrates a "festa major", which is a festival honoring the local patron saint or their history such as the Encamisada in Falset. They usually involve some kind of musical acts, activities for children, and of course gastronomic and wine fairs with tastings. To find out the exact dates and program of each festa major, visit the Priorat Tourism website or ask at the office they have in Falset.
www.turismepriorat.org

Nit de les Garnatxes in Capçanes
This is a big event that coincides with being on the Friday of the Priorat Wine Fair in Falset which is the first weekend in May. Held inside Celler de Capçanes, the cost for entrance is typically 15€ and allows attendees to taste a variety of Grenache wines each bottled to showcase one of the soil types that are found in the area. Its sister event, the Nit de les Carinyenes is the same, but in Porrera and focusing on the Carignan grape. While one is three hours before the other, it's virtually impossible to visit both.

Fira de l'oli de la baronia in Cabacés
To celebrate the year's new olive oil, they have a fair in the first week of December to show the history of olive production as well as all the methods used.

Festa de l'oli in Ulldemolins
In December, the village puts on this event to celebrate the arrival of the "oli nou" or the olive oil that's just been pressed. They organize a big mid-morning breakfast with all manner of dishes incorporating the new oil.

Festa de la Truita amb Suc in Ulldemolins
This festival pays tribute to the very delicious and signature "juicy omelet" that they make in the region. It happens each year on the second Sunday of March.

El Tast de Blancs
On the Friday of the Falset Wine Fair in May, the Aguiló brothers (who own the two main wine shops in town) put on a tasting of the white wines of Priorat as well as a few from outside the region. A grand event for white wine lovers or those who didn't know this other side of the wines from the region.

Fira del Vi

Suggested Itineraries

To decide which of the 50+ DO Montsant wineries to visit in a short period of time can be a daunting endeavor. The following are a few suggested schedules for people wishing to visit the region for two days or a weekend. These serve merely as a starting point though and within each of the sub regions in the following section, one day options are given as well. Note that most if not all wineries require prior reservations for visits, so reference the cellars section in the guide to plan accordingly.

The Highlights
Start out the day with a visit to the cooperative of Falset-Marçà. This cooperative offers a great entry point to the wines of DO Montsant as well as the wonderful Art Nouveau architecture that defines this historic cellar. Have lunch at el Celler de l'Àspic and bathe in its incredible wine list. Head to Capafons-Ossó for an afternoon visit with a small, family winery. Stay the night at Hostal Sport or, if you prefer to experience the Catalan "casa rural" stay at Casa Fontanals just outside of Falset. Have dinner at Hostal Sport or El Cairat.

For the second day, go to up to La Figuera and visit Ficaria Vins to taste what wonderful things they do with Grenache up there. Make sure to visit the Ermita de Sant Pau just outside of the village. When coming back, pass through El Masroig and have lunch at Restaurant Nou 21. After lunch go to Capçanes and have a visit at Vinyes Domènech. Once finished, grab a bite at Lo Casal before heading home or spending another night.

Wine Families
One of the most important aspects to DO Montsant are the families that have been making wine there for generations. Experience this by starting out the day with a visit to Vermunver in Marçà. Once finished have lunch at the very tasty Celler La Miloquera or La Sènia. After lunch head to El Masroig and visit Coca i Fitó to experience the new style of wines these brothers are making or the classic cooperative of families at Celler El Masroig. Have dinner at one of the restaurants in Falset. Stay at either Mas Figueres in Marçà or the budget option of Cal Benito in Capçanes.

Begin the next day with a visit to Vinyes d'en Gabriel who have been making wine in Darmós forever. Have lunch at Restaurant Nou 21 in El Masroig and continue on the very scenic drive to Cabacés for a visit at Mas de les Vinyes who are a winemaking family in the small village on the western fringe of the region. When coming back, pass through Gratallops and have dinner at La Boca del Llop.

Enjoy the Ride, Leave the Car
You can indeed visit DO Montsant without a car, but it requires planning and you're best off being based in Falset. Call Capafons-Ossó to arrange a visit and let them know when you're arriving so they can pick you up at the nearby Marçà-Falset train station. Enjoy the visit of their winery in the morning. Afterwards have them drop you off at Hostal Sport to leave your bags and enjoy lunch. In the afternoon, pop across the street to the Falset-Marçà cooperative for a visit, buying wines from their shop or Vins i Olis next door. Go have a drink at Calaix de Sastre and have dinner at Celler de l'Àspic or possibly Quinoa.

Catch the shuttle to Marçà and visit Vermunver in the morning followed by lunch at either Celler La Miloquera or La Sènia. In the afternoon, schedule a visit to either Dos Terras just outside of Marçà or take the shuttle back to Falset for a visit with Alfredo Arribas.

Make sure to leave enough time to catch the last train from Marçà-Falset station or spend another night, take the bus down to Capçanes, visit Celler de Capçanes in the morning and take the train from there.

The Grand Old Cooperatives
One of the most fascinating aspects of this region (and the reason people were able to survive) were the big wine and oil cooperatives that were formed in the early 20th century. They're still functioning and many can be visited today.

Start the day in Celler de Capçanes for their tour and tasting and grab a coffee at Lo Casal afterwards. Then head to El Masroig, have lunch at Nou 21 and afterwards visit Celler El Masroig. Spend the night at Hostal Sport in Falset and have dinner there or Celler de l'Àspic. The next morning enjoy a visit to the art nouveau cellar of Ètim, the Falset-Marçà cooperative. Afterwards take a drive up to Cornudella and have lunch at Fonda del Racó then visit their cooperative which was created by the same architect as Falset-Marçà but in a different style. Pay a visit to Siurana in the evening and if around in April, go to the fair of the cooperatives at Castell del Vi in Falset.

Zones

Cabacés, La Figuera, El Molar

El Masroig, Darmós, La Serra d'Almos

Els Guiamest, Capçanes, Marçà

Falset, Pradell de la Teixeta

Cornudella de Montsant, Siurana, Ulldemolins

WINERIES

1. Mas de les Vinyes
2. Agrícola Aubacs i Solans
3. Ficaria VIns
4. Grifoll Declara
5. Orto Vins
6. Can Blau

SITES

1. Museu a l'aire lliure
2. Pont de Cavaloca
3. L'Ermita de Sant Pau
4. Coves de Rogerals

AMENITIES

1. Ca l'Aleixa
2. Ca Calbert
3. Ca la Mari
4. Cal Llop/La Boca
5. Cal Mateu
6. Cal Trucafort
7. Neus
8. Perxe
9. El Racó de La Figuera
10. El Racó de la Finestra

- Municipality
- River
- Road
- Secondary road
- Wineries
- Sites
- Amenities

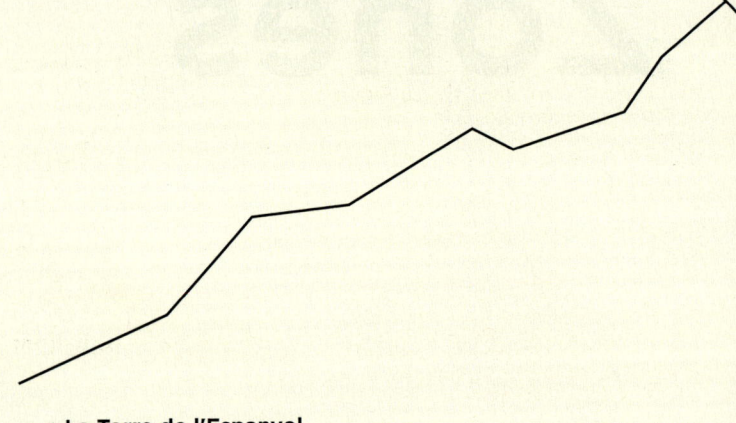

◄ **La Torre de l'Espanyol**

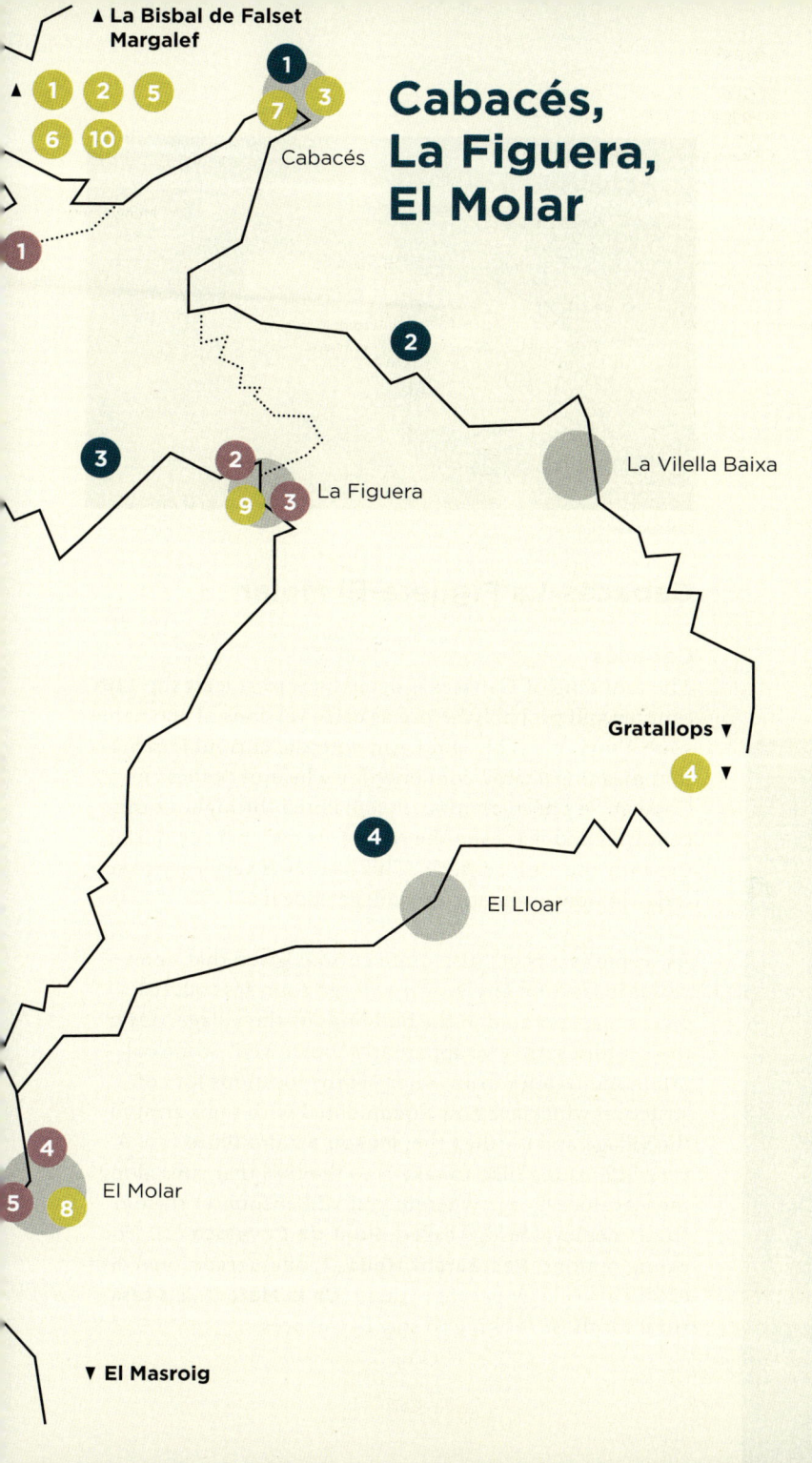

Cabacés

Cabacés-La Figuera-El Molar

Cabacés
The founding of Cabacés is dated back to at least the 13th century and probably before as early versions of the name were a mix of Arabic and Latin with the current incarnation meaning a large container for wheat or "cabàs" in Catalan. It's been continually inhabited throughout the centuries and was even the seat of its own barony during the 13th and 14th century. This history is very easy to see today in how authentic the village appears.

As scenic as it is, it's also quite curious given that upon closer inspection any visitor will see countless oddball pieces incorporated in the buildings of the village. Over the centuries, they've apparently "borrowed" stone columns and façades from other nearby locations for construction which are now documented with signs around the village and is called the, **Museu a l'aire lliure** (1). A very interesting hike to take is to the trail that runs along the Cavaloca Gorge wherein you will encounter the old stone medieval bridge called, **Pont de Cavaloca** (2). For eating options, **Restaurant Neus** (7) offers traditional dishes and a weekday prix fixe menu. **Ca la Mari** (3) is a casa rural for those looking to stay in Cabacés.

Further up the road from Cabacés are La Bisbal de Falset and Margalef. While not having any wineries, they're popular bases for rock climbing in the area and thus have a number of hotels such as: **Ca l'Aleixa** (1), **Cal Mateu** (5), and **Cal Trucafort** (6) (also a decent restaurant) in La Bisbal and **Ca Calbert** (2) and **El Racó de la Finestra** (10) in Margalef. For the adventurous and curious, they're a pleasant detour.

La Figuera

It's a steep ascent to reach the 575m altitude of La Figuera, but it's quite worth it as the view from the village is incredible and with a must-see stop at the **Ermita de Sant Pau** (3) nearby you can see seven different provinces of Spain on a clear day including a view up to the Pyrenees, a very distant 120km away.

The town quite simply takes its name from "fig tree" in Catalan which has been the official name since the 14th century. The legend is that historically there was a massive fig tree where the village is today that Roman shepherds sheltered their herds under.

It's a unique village as it sits atop a mountain range with valleys sloping on each side. This unique landscape makes the Grenache grapes grown here either the best in DO Montsant or simply, "unique" depending upon who you talk to. For meals, there is **El Racó de La Figuera** (9) which offers local dishes.

El Molar

Old ruins dating from 600BC are very close to el Molar and show the founding of the village to be from antiquity with a Roman origin. The name is thought to be derived from the word for "mill" and referred to those that were in the area, constructed from the red sandstone that's abundant up in the Montsant cliffs.

Serving as a crossroads for the area to other villages, it was part of the neighboring Garcia municipality until the mid-19th century. These days, the 300 or so residents make a living the same way as they have for generations via wine, oil, and almonds. For those looking to stay in El Molar, **Perxe** (8) offers a casa rural with space for up to 12 people and a different Catalan writer in residence each month.

Suggested Itinerary
Drive to La Figuera via El Molar and make a morning visit to **Ficaria Vins**. Go visit the **Ermita de Sant Pau** and the incredible view. Go to lunch at **Neus** in Cabacés and pay an afternoon visit to **Mas de les Vinyes**.

The Gratallops and Les Vilelles sections in our DOQ Priorat guide offer additional nearby cellars, sites, and restaurants to combine with a visit to this zone.

Contacts

Ca l'Aleixa
977819340, 629342893
Major, 19
La Bisbal de Falset
www.calaleixa.com

Ca Calbert
977819321, 607264841
Baix, 12
Margalef
www.cacalbet.com

Ca la Mari
933454031, 696917736
Balmes, 8
Cabacés
www.calamari.es

Cal Llop/La Boca del Llop
977839502
De dalt, 21
Gratallops
www.cal-llop.com

Cal Mateu
977819185, 687467963
Major, 29
La Bisbal de Falset
www.calmateu.es

Cal Trucafort
977819374, 686989585
Major, 12
La Bisbal de Falset
www.caltrucafort.com

La Figuera

Museu a l'aire lliure
Cabacés
www.cabaces.com

Neus
977054745, 675329169
Puntarré, 1
Cabacés
www.restaurantneus.com

Perxe
977825504, 670544420
De la Font
El Molar

El Racó de La Figuera
977402490, 650900927
Carretera de La Figuera
La Figuera

El Racó de la Finestra
977819008, 677611098
Carretera, 7
Margalef

WINERIES

1. Mas de la Abundància
2. Celler El Masroig
3. Coca i Fitó
4. Vinyes d'en Gabriel
5. Joan d'Anguera
6. Anguera Domènech
7. Cairats
8. Aibar
9. Cedó Anguera
10. Agrícola de La Serra d'Almos

SITES

1. L'Ermita Les Pinyeres

AMENITIES

1. Allotjament Rural Rosa Vernet
2. Ca la Lola
3. Casal Flor de Maig
4. Mas d'Alerany
5. Restaurant Nou 21

- Municipality
- River
- Road
- Secondary road
- Wineries
- Sites
- Amenities

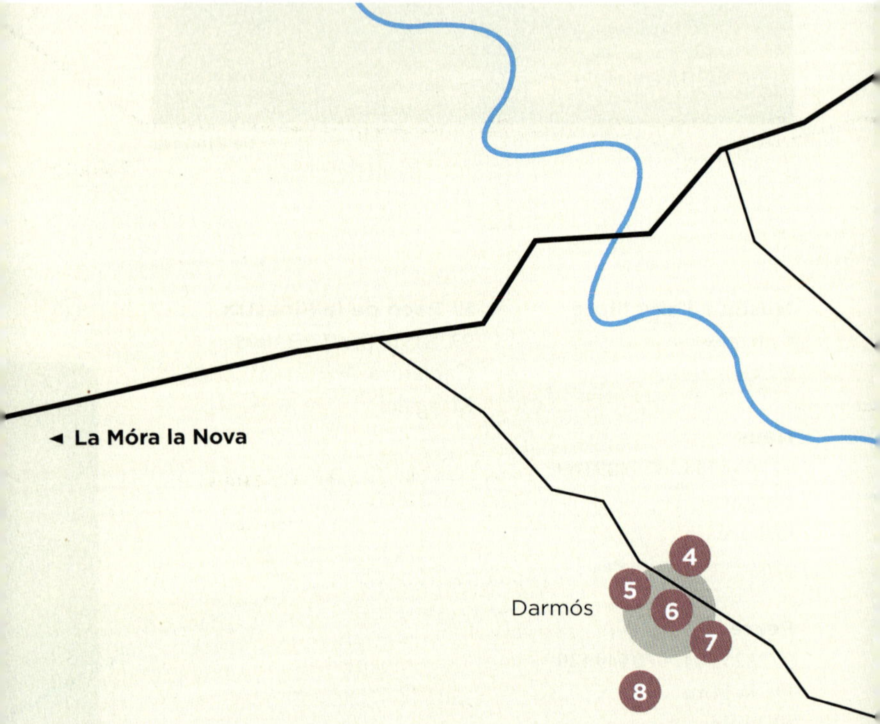

◄ La Móra la Nova

Darmós

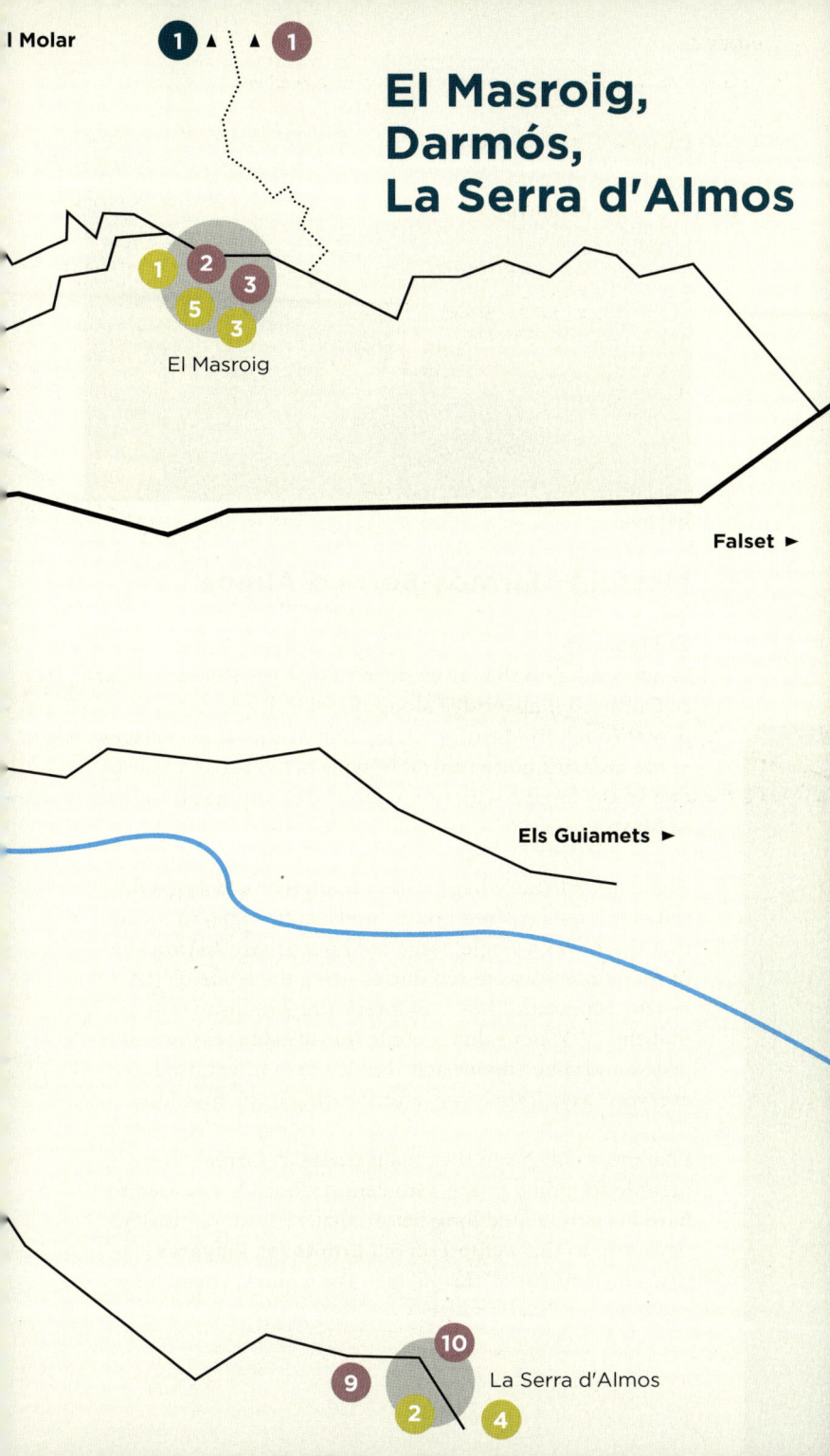

Darmós

Masroig-Darmós-Serra d'Almos

El Masroig
While sitting on the far western side of the Priorat comarca and straddling a ridge along the hills, it's hard not to pass through El Masroig. Being one of the larger villages in the area, it's quite central to wine activities and houses one of the largest wineries in all of DO Montsant, Celler El Masroig.

The name of this village is easy to understand as in Old Catalan it means, "red house" and can be taken to mean that there was a single, large red house there historically or many homes were red due to using the stone of the nearby Montsant Bluff. An interesting linguistic note is that the "s" is not said for some inexplicable reason and it just sounds like "mahroach" but it's easy to get used to as everyone says it this way--after hearing it the first time.

Like most villages in the area it traces its formal, documented founding to the 13th century, but it's assumed to have been inhabited long before that. For more history, pay a trip to the well-preserved **Ermita les Pinyeres** (1) just a little north of the village. For a quick, cheap bite, stop in at the **Casal** (3). For a very tasty, very authentic village meal/experience eat at **Nou 21** (5) or hit it up when it switches to pub mode for the evening. For lodging, there's the rural house of **Rosa Vernet** (1).

Darmós
A bit out of the way in lower southwest of the region, the name of this village is thought to derive directly from an Arabic root that means, "the house of Moses". Whether this is true or not, the village is old, historic, home to many wineries and actually sits outside the Priorat comarca, but was wisely included in DO Montsant given the overall high quality of the wines they produce.

Quite lovely, it's set upon a hill that overlooks a large portion of the region with a wide ravine dropping off below it where many of the vineyards grow. Despite its scenic nature, it's sparsely populated and has just over 100 residents now.

La Serra d'Almos
This small village to the southeast of Darmós is actually an administrative part of the much larger village of Tivissa to the south. Historically, they've been known for their tasty bakeries. They also produce a good quantity of wine these days, but it's their olive oil that is one of the biggest attractions of this old village as they release it under the high quality DOP Siurana label. They have two casa rural options to stay at, **Ca la Lola** (2) and the 15th century masia, **Mas d'Alerany** (4).

Suggested Itinerary
Start out the day with a visit to a family cellar such as **Aibar** or **Cairats** and then stop in at the cooperative in **La Serra d'Almos** to taste and possibly buy their olive oils. Head up to El Masroig to have lunch at **Nou 21** and then visit **Celler El Masroig** to see wine production on a large scale. Finish out the day by seeing the late afternoon light and having a visit to the **Les Pinyeres** hermitage.

Contacts

Allotjament Rural Rosa Vernet
675423892
Passeig de l'Abre, 6
El Masroig

Ca la Lola
638840631
Escoles, 15
La Serra d'Almos
agroturismecalalola.blogspot.com

Casal Flor de Maig
977825424
Nou, 5
El Masroig

Mas d'Alerany
696761939
Escoles
La Serra d'Almos
www.masdalerany.com

Restaurant Nou 21
977825010
Nou, 21
El Masroig

El Masroig

WINERIES

1. Celler Els Guiamets
2. Mas de la Caçadora
3. Serra i Barceló
4. Celler de Capçanes
5. Vinyes Domènech
6. Clos Pissarra
7. Viñas del Montsant
8. Acústic
9. Vermunver
10. Portal del Montsant
11. Dos Terras
12. Vendrell Rived
13. Mas d'en Canonge

AMENITIES

1. Les Agulles/Estació de Falset-Marçà
2. Ca La Tieta Quima
3. Ca La Viola
4. Cal Benito
5. Cal Torner
6. Lo Casal Capçanenc
7. Celler La Miloquera
8. Estació de Capçanes
9. Mas Figueres
10. Mestral
11. La Plaça
12. La Sènia
13. La Vinya del Pare

- Municipality
- River
- Road
- Secondary road
- Wineries
- Sites
- Amenities

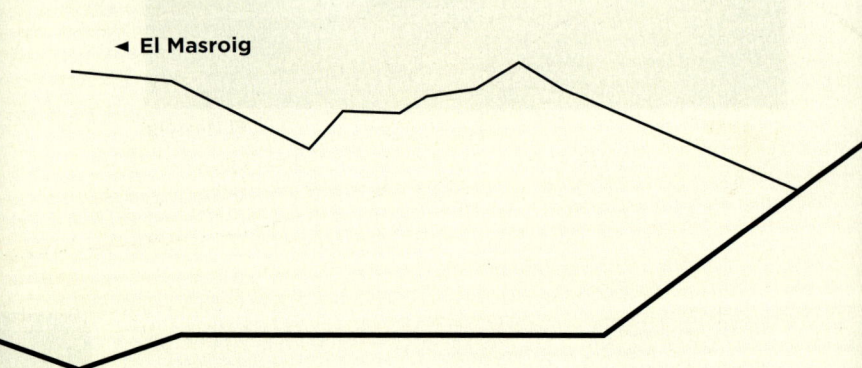

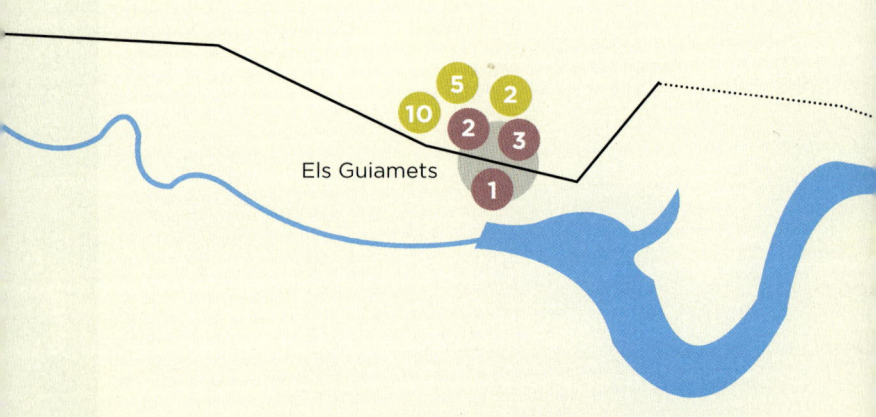

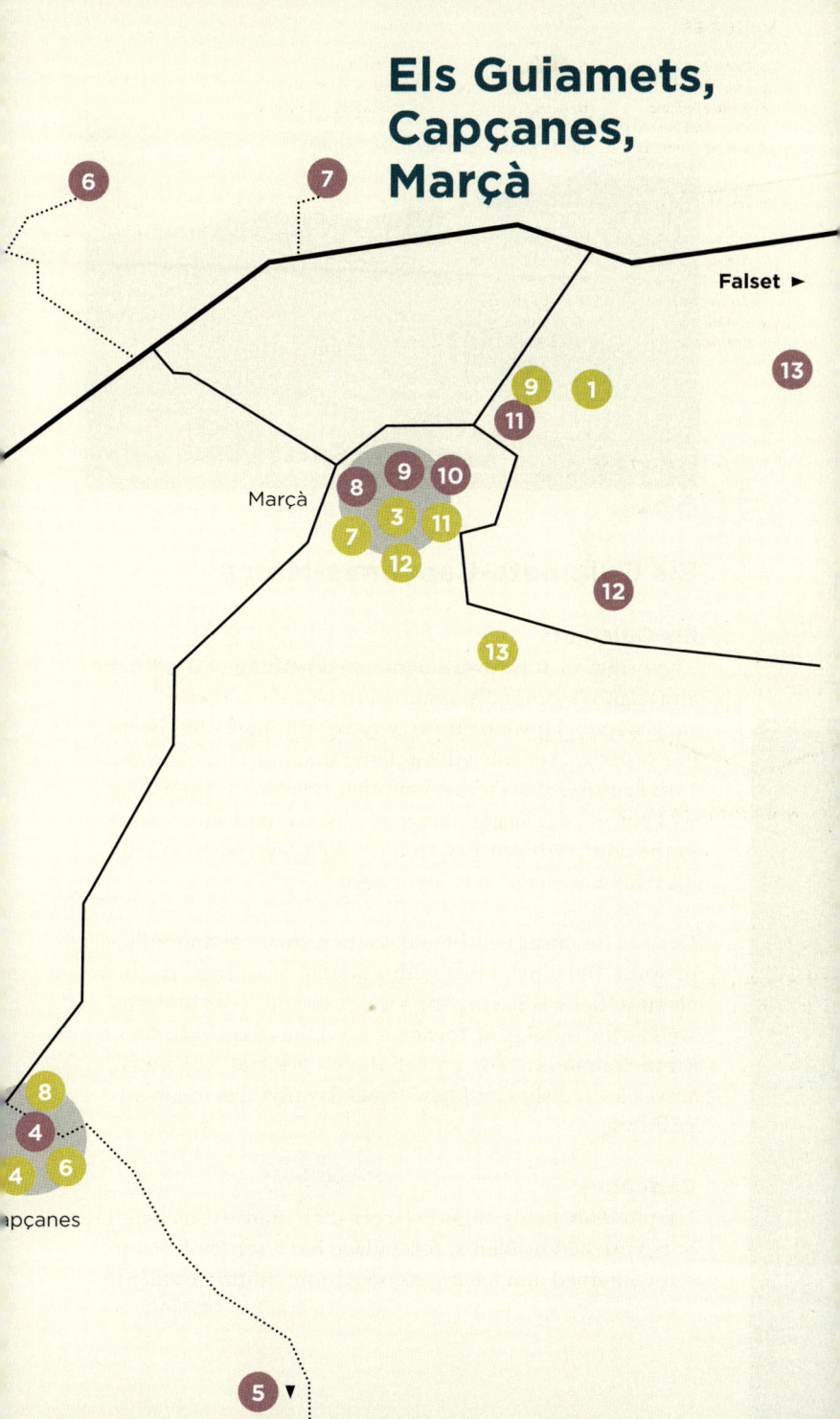

Capçanes

Els Guiamets-Capçanes-Marçà

Els Guiamets
The origin of this town's name is something of a mystery although it's generally assumed to be a derivative of a person's name. However it came to be, this name has been in existence ever since documents stated it as such in the 13th century. This creates another mystery as the village was part of the larger village of Tivissa until some point in the later 19th century (and it's unknown when exactly) it became a village in its own right.

Despite the intrigue, these days it's a small, quaint village of some 300 inhabitants with a couple of cellars. Its main claim to fame is having the local reservoir in its limits as well as the hotel, **Cal Torner** (5) and the casa rural, **Ca La Tieta Quima** (2). For a meal, there's **Mestral** (10) which serves local dishes and has a weekday prix fixe menu all year long.

Capçanes
Despite only being slightly larger than many of its neighbors with 400 residents, this village has a sense of being self-contained and having its own momentum. Evidence

shows that it's been inhabited since the Iron Age and the first documents of it exist from the 12th-13th centuries following the re-conquest of the region from Moorish control.

Theories about the name abound but it's thought to have been derived from the older Catalan word "capçar" which meant to place flat stones in an area. Stone placing aside, the most historically significant person from the village to date was Pere Joan Barceló i Anguera, known as "Carrasclet" who was a coal seller that became a Catalan resistance fighter in the early 18th century. They have a statue of him in a small park at the entrance to the village.

Despite its size, the village has both a good casa rural to stay at called, **Cal Benito** (4) as well as the **Casal** (6) to eat at. The latter of which is a generally lively spot where most everyone in the village passes at some point in the day especially the cellar workers when they're done with their shifts. Generally a good spot to get a drink or snack, they have quite tasty food on Fridays and Saturdays.

Marçà

While it is one of the larger villages in the Priorat comarca, it's still surprising to find that this village holds a great deal of history, most of it focusing on the large, 60m hill that rises up directly behind it called Miloquera. Most likely inhabited since the Paleolithic Era, the name of the village is thought to derive from Latin and the Roman god of war, Mars. Roman ruins have been found in the area as well as the ruins of a Moorish castle that stood at the top of the hill in the 9th century.

In more recent times, there was a Marçà Castle from the 12th century as well which doesn't exist anymore but eventually led to a monastery being founded in the early 17th century which still stands today at the entrance to town, but has been deserted for 300 years.

The village is well appointed in food options with **Celler La Miloquera** (7) offering excellent meals, **La Sènia** (12) being a tasty spot for lunch, and **La Plaça** (11) being good for a local meal as well as **Les Agulles** (1) at the train station. For lodging there's the casa rural **Ca La Viola** (3), **La Vinya del Pare** (13), and the very nice hotel, **Mas Figueres** (9).

Suggested Itinerary
Start with a visit to **Celler de Capçanes** and take in their large yet delicious production. Or alternatively go to **Vinyes Domènech** to see a unique family approach to winemaking. Have lunch in Marçà at either **Celler La Miloquera** or **La Sènia** and then pay a visit to **Vermunver** in the afternoon. Pop back over to Capçanes in the late afternoon to share a beer with the locals at **Lo Casal** if you want a taste of actual modern village life.

Contacts

Les Agulles
977178215, 610269686
Estació de Marçà-Falset
Marçà

Ca La Tieta Quima
977413109, 619128203
Sant Lluís, 8
Els Guiamets
www.calatietaquima.cat

Ca La Viola
977178288, 669565651
Dalt, 18
Marçà
www.calaviola.org

Cal Benito
977830894, 620314808
Font, 12
Capçanes
www.calbenito.cat

Cal Torner
977413052, 659251766
Raval, 4
Els Guiamets
www.caltorner.com

Lo Casal Capçanenc
Pau Casals, 51
Capçanes
blocs.tinet.cat/locasal/

Celler La Miloquera
977178075
Bassa, 10
Marçà

Mas Figueres
977178011, 687814144
Carretera Falset-Marçà,
Km 2
Marçà
www.masfigueres.com

Mestral
977413073
Carretera, 53
Els Guiamets

La Plaça
977178002
Plaça de les Arenes, 3
Marçà

La Sènia
977178003
Baixada de la Font, 3
Marçà

La Vinya del Pare
977178346, 677708115
Carretera Marçà-La Torre de
Fontaubella, Km 1.4
Marçà
www.mothersgarden.org

Marçà

WINERIES

1. Capafons-Ossó
2. Laurona
3. Alfredo Arribas
4. Mas Sersal
5. Ètim
6. Venus La Universal
7. Escola d'Enologia Jaume Ciurana
8. Pascona
9. Sant Rafel
10. Vitec

WINE SHOPS

1. Vins i Olis del Priorat
2. Vinateria Aguiló

SITES

1. L'Ermita de Sant Gregori
2. Castell del Vi
3. Celler Cooperatiu Falset Marçà

AMENITIES

1. El Cairat
2. Cal Cabré
3. Cal Porxo
4. Casa Fontanals
5. El Celler de l'Àspic
6. Entrepà i Pa
7. Quinoa
8. Hostal Sport
9. Calaix de Sastre
10. Estació de Falset-Marçà

- Municipality
- River
- Road
- Secondary road
- Wineries
- Sites
- Amenities
- Wine Shops

▲ Gratallops

◄ Bellmunt

◄ Marçà

Falset, Pradell de la Teixeta

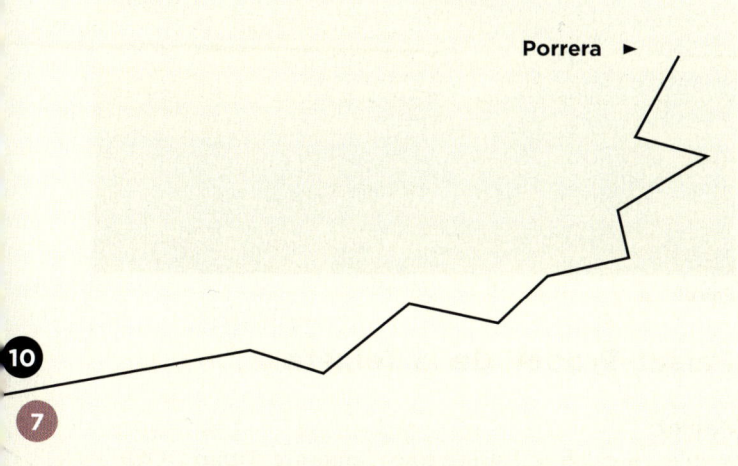

Porrera ►

10
7

8

4

2 3 ►

9 ►

Falset

Pradell de la Teixeta / Reus ►

1

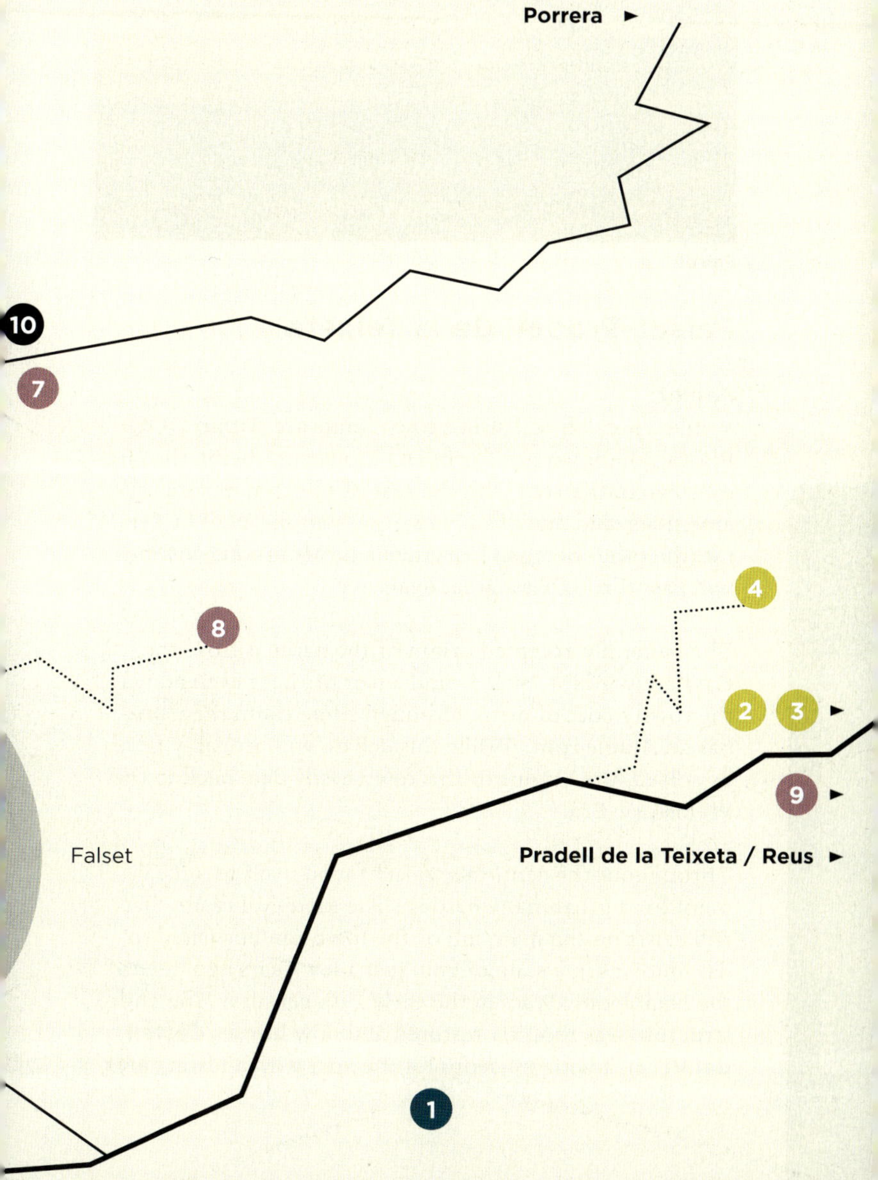

Falset

Falset-Pradell de la Teixeta

Falset

While a portion of Falset's town limits are within DOQ Priorat, the town itself is in DO Montsant. Being the largest town in the area with the seat of the comarca, many amenities, and one of only two gas stations in all of Priorat (the other being in Cornudella de Montsant), visitors will pass through it a great deal.

The generally accepted origin of the name is from the Catalan word for "sickle" and a pair of them even adorn the town's coat of arms, although some claim the name has an Arabic root. While this debate will probably never be solved, the origins of this town easily date back to the Prehistoric Era.

Throughout the centuries, Falset found itself as a focal point for a great many battles. The Medieval castle that still exists on the main hill of the town can be visited today, but was in a state of ruin just a few years ago due to the Napoleonic Wars in the early 19th century. The entire structure was recently restored and now houses **Castell del Vi** (2), a wine museum for the area with a tasting area and frequent events. Also interesting is the **Ermita de Sant Gregori** (1) which is on the other side of the main road in to Falset. Dug out of a sandstone cliff, it's especially impressive at sunset.

The largest hotel in the region with 18 rooms is **Hostal Sport** (8) which also has a restaurant and an extensive wine list from the region. For general, basic eating, **Entrepà i Pa** (6) across from Hostal Sport offers simple sandwiches at a good price for the budget minded. The restaurants, **El Cairat** (1), **Quinoa** (7), and **El Celler de l'Àspic** (5) offer the best higher end options to be found, although the service at Quinoa leaves much to be desired. El Celler de l'Àspic is especially noteworthy for its extensive local and international (mainly French) wine list and the owner's extensive knowledge about wine, as well as exquisitely crafted modern cuisine. And for a great wine bar showing off the region, stop in at **Calaix de Sastre** (9) who also feature tastings with regional winemakers on Sundays.

The two wines shops in Falset, **Vins i Olis del Priorat** (1) and **Vinateria Aguiló** (2) do the job of bringing the entire offer of wines to one spot. Almost every bottle made in the region can be found at either of these shops and at overall competitive prices, especially when compared to buying outside the region.

For those arriving by train, the **Marçà-Falset station** (10) is located about 2.2km southwest from the center of town making for an easy bike ride or a longer, but doable walk.

Pradell de la Teixeta

This small village is the first most will encounter when coming to the Priorat comarca. Just off the side of the road, it's a quiet, old town whose name means, "little field by the yew forest". While these days it's far overshadowed by other towns such as Falset, it was historically very prolific until the 14th century but plagues and other agricultural problems sent it in to a heavy decline to a point where it was nearly abandoned in the 16th century. Towards the end of the 19th century it had over 1,000 people living there, but again saw a steady decline leading up to an after the Spanish Civil War to the point today where it has about 200 residents.

Despite being right off the main road to Priorat, it's very quiet and tranquil, making for a decent getaway without going too deeply in to the region. For lodging it offers two very nice renovated old stone homes to stay in called, **Cal Cabré** (2) and **Cal Porxo** (3).

Suggested Itinerary
Plan the full morning around a visit to **Capafons-Ossó**. Have lunch at one of the restaurants in Falset such as **El Celler de l'Àspic** or **El Cairat**. Afterwards, pay a visit to either **Pascona** or **Ètim** and make sure hike just outside of Falset for the sunset at **Ermita de Sant Gregori** before grabbing a drink at **Calaix de Sastre**.

The Gratallops and Porrera sections in our DOQ Priorat guide offer additional nearby cellars, sites, and restaurants to combine with a visit to this zone.

Contacts

El Cairat
977830481, 620928618
Nou, 3
Falset
www.restaurantelcairat.com

Cal Porxo
977828243, 639350255
Major, 12
Pradell de la Teixeta
www.calporxo.com

Cal Cabré
664118325, 699803263
Major, 21
Pradell de la Teixeta
www.calcabre.com

Casa Fontanals
687465858, 637051662
Carretera 420, Km 844
Falset
www.fincafontanals.com

El Celler de l'Àspic
977831246
Miquel Barceló, 31
Falset
www.cellerdelaspic.com

Entrepà i Pa
977830294
Catalunya, 6
Falset

Quinoa
977830431
Miquel Barceló, 29
Falset
www.restaurantquinoa.com

Hostal Sport
977830078
Miquel Barceló, 4
Falset
www.hotelpriorat-hostalsport.com

Calaix de Sastre
687814144
Plaça de la Quartera, 39
Falset

Vinateria Aguiló
977830776
Miquel Barceló, 11
Falset
www.aguilo-prioratwines.com

Vins i Olis del Priorat
977831835
Miquel Barceló, 25
Falset
www.vinsiolisdelpriorat.com

Pradell de la Teixeta

WINERIES

1. Celler de l'Era
2. Cingles Blaus
3. Ronadelles
4. Baronia del Montsant
5. Celler Cooperatiu de Cornudella
6. Malondro
7. Noguerals
8. Graus de Siurana
9. Agrícola d'Ulldemolins Sant Jaume
10. Serra Major

SITES

1. Siurana
2. Celler Cooperatiu de Cornudella

AMENITIES

1. Apartment Montsant
2. Ca la Loreto
3. Cal Giral
4. Càmping Montsant Park
5. Càmping de Siurana
6. Casa Estivill
7. Fonda del Racó
8. Fonda Toldrà
9. Mirador de Siurana/El Carcaix
10. Mandrino Apts.
11. Mas del Salín
12. Molí del Pont
13. Pla del Castell
14. Lo Refugi/Xalet de l'Assut
15. Refugi d'Albarca
16. Refugi Ciriac Bonet
17. La Serra
18. Restaurant Siurana
19. La Siuranella
20. Els Tallers
21. Al Toll
22. Venta d'en Pubill
23. La Vileta

WINE SHOPS

1. Carnisseria Papió

- ● Municipality
- ━ River
- ━ Road
- ┈ Secondary road
- ● Wineries
- ● Sites
- ● Amenities
- ● Wine Shops

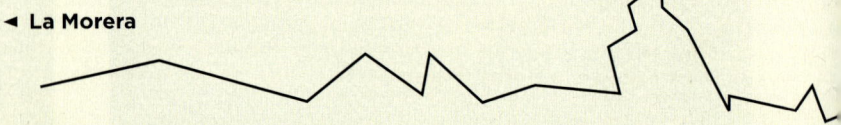

◀ **La Morera**

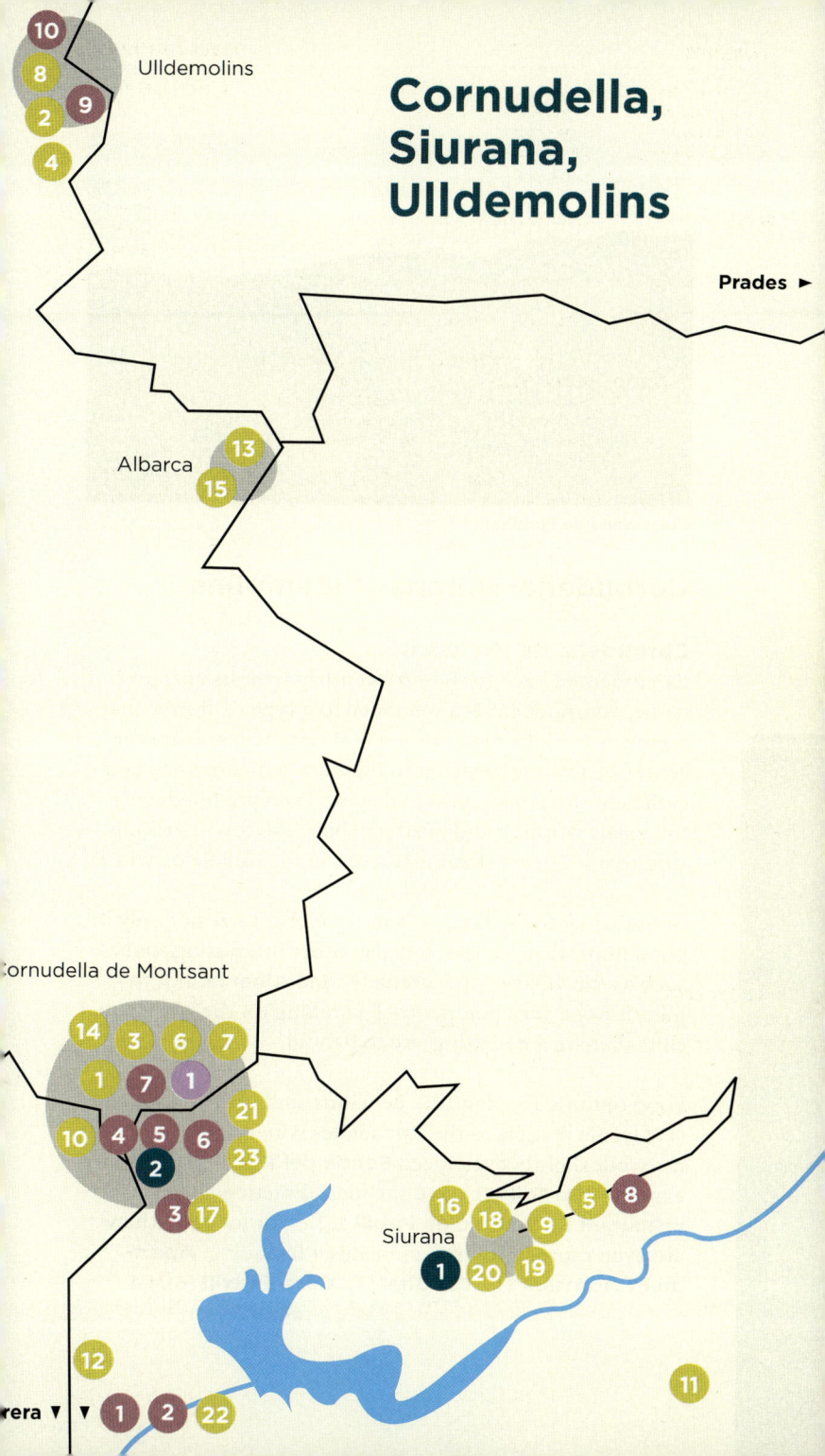

Cornudella de Montsant

Cornudella-Siurana-Ulldemolins

Cornudella de Montsant
Documented back to the 12th century with its current name, "cornudella" is a reference to a type of flower that is common in the area. Its general remoteness from the center of Priorat has led it to be more self-contained and sufficient than many other villages. Days are filled with the locals working and bustling about the town, making sure that it's never that quiet, even in the middle of winter.

Bounded by the striking Montsant bluffs it has not only a good number of cellars, but also other interesting spots such as the villages of **Siurana** (1) and **Albarca**, not to mention the very popular rock climbing on the Montsant cliffs that are a nailbiting site to behold.

Food options are plentiful, delicious, and include **La Serra** (17) (same owners as the Ronadelles winery), the very tasty but slightly overpriced **Fonda del Racó** (7), the more expensive **Al Toll** (21), and the local directional landmark/restaurant **La Venta d'en Pubill** (22). For lodging, there are even more options than in Falset including: **Apartment Montsant** (1), **Cal Giral** (3), **Casa Estivill** (6), **La**

Siurana

Vileta (23), the very basic, but incredibly affordable **Lo Refugi** (14), **Mandrino Apartments** (10), **Mas del Salín** (11), **Molí del Pont** (12), and **Xalet de l'Assut** (14). Also in nearby Albarca are, **Pla del Castell** (13) and **Refugi d'Albarca** (15) which also has a restaurant.

Siurana

Administratively, Siurana is part of Cornudella, but it's very important in its own right. A very historic settlement, it came under Moorish control somewhere around the 9th century and it was held until 1154 when it became the last village in Catalonia to be "reconquered". This led to the creation of the "Legend of the Moorish Queen" who supposedly threw herself off the cliffs upon seeing the Christian soldiers entering the village.

These days it's a steady draw for visitors for both the history and the stunning panoramic view out from the sharp cliffs that drop off its 757m altitude down to the Siurana Reservoir below. It's hard to believe that people have been able to live there for so long, but even now the village has 40 full time residents. Given its year-round tourism draw, much like Cornudella, it has a great wealth of food and lodging options. The restaurants of **El Carcaix** (9), **Mirador de Siurana**, **Els Tallers** (20), and the very popular **Sirurana** (18) are all good possibilities. For lodging there is **Càmping de Siurana** (5), the two star **La Siuranella** (19), and **Refugi Ciriac Bonet** (16) which is also a fantastic spot to have a drink on the edge of the cliff.

Ulldemolins
Originally a Moorish village that was built up for defense, it was "reconquered" in the middle of the 12th century as Christian forces moved southward. They rebuilt a great deal of the town over the centuries and it holds one of the very few examples in Catalonia of a Renaissance church that was built in the late 16th century. The name of this town, "eye of the windmills" seems curious at first until you learn that historically, there were eight water powered mills around the perimeter of the small plane where the village now sits at the center thus forming the "eye".

Given that the northern limit of the village is marked by "Purgatory Gorge" it gives a sense of the windswept and generally inhospitable environment that exists. But despite this, olive, grapes, and almonds all grow well. Due to the hiking trails and various natural sites in the area there are the lodging options of **Fonda Toldrà** (8) with affordable rooms and a restaurant with basic dishes, **Ca la Loreto** (2), and **Càmping Montsant Park** (4) which also has a bar and restaurant.

Suggested Itinerary
Start out the day with a visit to **Celler de l'Era**. Then fit in a visit to **Ronadelles** and have lunch at their **La Serra** restaurant, or eat at **Fonda del Racó**. In the afternoon visit **Baronia del Montsant** or the **Cooperative** and make sure to fit in enough time before sunset to visit **Siurana**.

The La Morera, Poboleda, and Porrera sections in our DOQ Priorat guide offer additional nearby cellars, sites, and restaurants to combine with a visit to this zone.

Contacts

Apartment Montsant
977821183, 648027811
Nou, 15-17
Cornudella de Montsant
www.apartamentosmontsant.com

Ca la Loreto
977561657, 626292979
Sant Bartomeu, 5
Ulldemolins
calaloreto.freshcreator.com

Cal Giral
977821082, 676647178
Sant Francesc, 1 &
Balç, 26-27
Cornudella de Montsant
www.calgiral.com

Càmping Montsant Park
977561708
Carretera Ulldemolins-
Cornudella, Km 0.5
Ulldemolins
www.campingmontsantpark.com

Càmping de Siurana
977821383, 629480602
Coll de Ginebre
Siurana
www.campingsiurana.com

Carnisseria Papió
977821157
Sant Francesc, 7
Cornudella de Montsant

Casa Estivill
977821032
Plaça de la Vila, 15
Cornudella de Montsant
www.casaestivill.com

Fonda del Racó
977 821 032
Plaça de la Vila, 10
Cornudella de Montsant
www.fondaelreco.com

Fonda Toldrà
977561537
Major, 33
Ulldemolins
www.fondatoldra.es

Mirador de Siurana/El Carcaix
977821472
Ctra. Cornudella-Siurana, Km 7
Siurana
www.miradordesiurana.cat

Mandrino Apartments
629170939
Comte de Rius, 4, 2-1
Cornudella de Montsant

Mas del Salín
699975557, 699975554
Carretera de l'Ermita de Sant Pau
Cornudella de Montsant
www.masdelsalin.com

Molí del Pont
607250492
Carretera Cornudella-Porrera, Km 2.5
Cornudella de Montsant
www.molidelpont.com

Pla del Castell
659863185
De la Plaça, 48
Albarca
www.pladelcastell.com

Lo Refugi/Xalet de l'Assut
977821313
Comte de Rius/Carretera Cornudella-Porrera
Cornudella de Montsant
www.montsantnatura.cat

Refugi d'Albarca
660660721
Plaça de la Vila
Albarca

Refugi Ciriac Bonet
977561409, 676883752
Pla de la Torre Alta
Siurana
www.facebook.com/refugi.siurana

La Serra
977821106
Carretera Cornudella-Porrera, Km 0.6
Cornudella de Montsant
www.restaurantlaserra.com

Restaurant Siurana
977821027
Major
Siurana
www.restaurantsiurana.com

La Siuranella
977821144
Rentadors
Siurana
www.siuranella.com

Els Tallers
977821144, 630871462
Rentadors
Siurana
www.restaurantelstallers.net

Al Toll
636108235
Compte De Rius 8
Cornudella de Montsant

La Venta d'en Pubill
977821077
Intersection C-242 & T-702
Cornudella de Montsant

La Vileta
977821006
Vileta, 16 A
Cornudella de Montsant
www.lavileta.net

Ulldemolins

Cellars

DO Montsant

Garage

 64

 225

albert | Jordi | david | Raul | Noe
jose | Jose | Navarro | Jose | Badi
Huerta | Ruiz | Batra | Ruiz | mor

Albert Jané Úbeda
owner & enolog

GPS
41.127694
0.798823

Acústic
Marçà, *Carrer de Progrès*

Visits: They are offered on a limited basis. Call ahead to see if an appointment can be made.
Contact: 629472988 | acustic@acusticceller.com
Website: www.acusticceller.com
Languages: English

Albert Jané Úbeda set out to make his name in DO Montsant starting in 2003 with his first vintage in 2004 from several old vineyards he had purchased in the region. He wasn't unfamiliar to wine before arriving there as seen in his first last name that shows his relation to the Jané Ventura family who is a big producer up in Penedès and is where he received his initiation to winemaking.

In his compact, functional cellar that used to be a textile factory just outside of Marçà on the road to Capçanes he is now making about 100,000 bottles a year from the 28ha comprised only of local grape varietals including the rarely seen Grey Grenache. For anyone who has tasted his wines, his approach is readily apparent given that he uses no new oak and does his best to express the region in each bottle. Albert creates something of a DO Montsant Melting Pot with his wines as he makes use of vineyards from all over the region, selecting from the various microclimates spread about this crescent shaped region. While he started in neighboring Els Guiamets, his vines are from multiple villages including the rather far flung Cornudella. All of them he visits on a regular basis.

His naming scheme is curious as most wineries make their highest end wine be the namesake of the winery. With Acústic, it's actually the base wine that carries the name as Albert finds it a fitting for the wine that started his whole endeavor. It also offers a great price-quality ratio that's earned these wines a lot of fans. In the last few years, he's been using the approach of Acústic for his new project in neighboring DOQ Priorat called, Ritme which keeps with the musical theme he uses in all his wines.

Rosat 2012
An interesting mix of fresh red fruits and floral aromas with minor herbal notes in the nose. The body is fresh and absorbing with a persistent finish.

Grenache, Grey Grenache, Carignan

13.5% | 10€

Blanc 2011
Has a chalky nose with golden apples and white floral aromas. The body is intense, but perfectly balanced while being very pleasing with a long finish.

White Grenache, Grey Grenache, Macabeu, Xarel·lo

13.5% | 12.50€

Negre 2011
Toasted almonds, smokiness, and a touch of dark chocolate to the nose. The body is balanced with dusty plum notes as well as leather and chocolate. Red fruits drift in to the finish with the acidity coming up a bit more just at the end.

Carignan, Grenache

14% | 12.50€

Braó 2011
A spicy nose of toasted almond, waffle, and a little vanilla as well as dark blackberry. This spice carries in to the body with slight touches of leather. Mineral elements appear as well with some blueberry notes. Elegant with a large soul.

Grenache, Carignan

15% | 24€

Auditori 2010

Aromas of red fruits such as wild strawberries and jammy plums along with cocoa, vanilla, and orange peel. The body is elegant, delicate, round, and sweet with a finish that brings up the cocoa notes in more detail.

100% Grenache

15% | 45€

GPS
41.216895
0.728584

Agrícola Aubacs i Solans
La Figuera, *Carretera de La Figuera, 1*

Visits: While not open for visits, their shop is open Sundays in the morning.
Contact: 977825228,606366250 | aubacs.i.solans@wanadoo.es

Life in Priorat is not easy and in a remote village like La Figuera, even more so. It's for this reason that in 1932 a group of 15 farmers formed a cooperative for the village to produce their olive oil and wine. Over time, more people joined and it reached its maximum amount of members around 25-30 years ago. Since then, it's been in a bit of a decline.

In the 1980s people left to produce their own wines and people from outside the area were coming in and buying the old vineyards. Added in to that, others decided to retire as farming the lands around this village is hard work and today there are about 12 members (with three truly active) of the cooperative producing grapes and about 30 producing olives.

Their cellar is a straightforward affair with a barrel aging room below the main area that can only be reached by a ladder. From this they produce about 10,000 bottles a year and sell a great deal more as bulk wine. Most of their production is Grenache with a bit of Merlot and Cabernet Sauvignon as part of the mix.

View from La Figuera with fog

🔴 **Jove 2012**
Caramel notes in the nose as well as a fresh acidity and dark fruits. While a bit gaunt, green, and light in the body it carries pleasant notes of the fruits out in the finish.
Grenache, Merlot, Cab Sauvignon
15% | 3.20€

🔴 **Selecció 2011**
Toasted aromas along with leather, dried tea leaves, and cured cherries. The body is generally well-balanced with delicate red fruit flavors that lead in to a finish that's somewhat short.
Grenache, Merlot, Cab Sauvignon
14.25% | 5.15€

🔴 **Prosit 2009**
Discreet and elegant in the nose with touches of leather, minerality, and cured red fruits such as a cherry. In the body it's very smooth and elegant, presenting an easy to drink wine with a lingering, persistent, dry finish that could easily age for another five years.
100% Grenache
14.5% | 10.40€

Ivan Sales Pérez
president

GPS
41.08035
0.745648

Agrícola de La Serra d'Almos
La Serra d'Almos, *Avinguda de La Cooperativa*

Visits: Call ahead to arrange a full visit. Their shop is open daily, in the mornings.
Contact: 977418125 | coopserra@telefonica.net
Website: www.serradalmos.com

In 2013, this cooperative celebrated 50 years of existence. Like most in the area, it was created by the farmers in the village to produce both wines and olive oil as a group thus lessening the risks and improving their commercial viability. While it was founded in 1963, they didn't actually start construction on the building they currently occupy until three harvests later utilizing large underground tanks of 25-28,000 liters that were built for wine production and that they still use today. Of course they've been lined with resin now for clean wine production and the volume is augmented by additional stainless steel tanks.

For over 25 years all of the wines that they produced were sold in bulk. Bottling began in 1979 as shown by a bottle that they keep in their barrel-aging room. Like the other wineries in the area, they automatically switched from DO Tarragona to DO Montsant in 2002 and what their labels lack in cutting edge design, they counter with being very affordable.

Today they have about 80 associates between the olive and wine production. An amusing, easygoing group of farmers alongside the wines they also produce one of the finest olive oils in the region under with DOP Siurana certification.

Various bottles both full and empty in their archive

🔴 Mussefres Rosat 2012
Candied cherries to the nose with some minor earthy notes and pomegranate. The body is medium strength with decent balance. The finish brings back the cherry notes as well as a touch of pepper.

100% Grenache

13% | 4.50€

🟡 Mussefres Blanc 2012
Generally citric in the nose with grapefruit notes that lead in to a generally even body and a somewhat herbal finish with minor notes touched of white flowers.

Macabeu, White Grenache

13% | 4.50€

🔴 Mussefres Negre 2012
Strong notes of acidity on the nose as well as some blackberry and wheat. The body isn't terribly well-balanced and finishes quite abruptly.

Carignan, Grenache, Syrah

13.3% | 4.50€

🔴 Mussefres Criança 2009
Touches of strawberry to the nose along with balsamic notes and some oxidation. Light and dry in the body, this character carries in to the finish as well.

Grenache, Carignan, Tempranillo, Cab Sauvignon

14% | 8€

🔴 Fidel 2008
A separate project by the enolog, the nose has minor hazelnut elements and is light overall and not terrible defined. The body is overall smooth but without strong notes other than round red fruits with a dry finish.

Grenache, Carignan

14% | 8€

AGRÍCOLA DE LA SERRA D'ALMOS

GPS
41.320727
0.880716

Agrícola d'Ulldemolins Sant Jaume
Ulldemolins, *Carrer de Saltadora, 17*

Visits: While they have no visits, their shop is open Saturday, Sunday, and holidays.
Contact: 977561640,977561613 | info@coopulldemolins.com
Website: www.coopulldemolins.com

When looking out upon the far northern reaches of Priorat where the cooperative of Ulldemolins calls home, it's easy to see why the farmers in the area would band together. The landscape is rough, unforgiving and at a relatively high altitude with the lowest point in the village being 600m. It's also a unique microclimate and all of the 150 associates of the cooperative have vines, olives, and nuts of varying amounts that they've produced together since 1953.

Initially they only sold bulk wines. While they still sell a great deal of their wines this way, since 2003 (basically since the formation of DO Montsant) they've evolved and now bottle about a third of their production as well which totals around 10,000 bottles in a good year.

While they produce about 60,000 liters of wine a year, their main enterprise up there are the olives and they produce a very high quality oil under the DOP Siurana certification. It's incredibly popular as seen when visiting any weekend during opening hours for the shop. Weekenders from all over Catalonia hungrily buy up several five liter jugs of their organic olive oil to take home, especially when the newly pressed and intensely aromatic, new oil is available.

An old olive press with the rugged mountains behind

🟡 **Les Pedrenyeres Blanc 2012**
Fresh with white flowers and chalkiness to the nose. The body is pleasant and rich in the mouth. Lightly smoky and dry in the finish with light fruit notes.
White Grenache, Macabeu
13.5% | 10€

🔴 **Ulldemolins Garnatxa 2012**
Dark cherries and blackberries are in the nose along with some citric notes such as orange peel. The body isn't heavily structured and the tannins are a bit pronounced. The finish trails off with the tannins and while not terrible long, is pleasant.
100% Grenache
14% | 4.50€

🔴 **Les Pedrenyeres Criança 2011**
Dark, smoky fruits in the nose along with alcoholic notes. Quite dry in the body, it's somewhat lacking in overall volume ending in a dry finish with notes of blackberries.
100% Grenache
15.5% | 10€

Jaume Pinyol
Toni Freixes
owners

GPS
41.095015
0.702741

Aibar

Darmós, *Barranc de Nolla de Darmós*

Visits: Call or email ahead to schedule a visit and tasting at a price of 3€ per person. Larger groups can be accommodated.
Contact: 977417532,639321367 | tofresan@yahoo.es,celleraibar@agricoles.org
Website: www.celleraibar.eu
Languages: English, French

Any quick glimpse at a map will show the small valley that the village of Darmós hovers above to be teeming with dirt roads zigzagging everywhere. Amidst all these potential routes is the Aibar cellar. While the locals will probably tell you differently, those who are newcomers to this village will find the easiest route is via the last dirt road you come upon when exiting the village. From there you'll drop down to the floor of the valley and the old property that Jaume Pinyol's family has been farming for ages.

This is the best way to sum up the history of the cellar as, like most families in DO Montsant, Jaume doesn't have an exact time as to when they started making wine. He simply states that they pretty much always have as long as his family has lived in the village which, much like the winemaking goes back to times unknown. Up until 2005, all of the wines were produced in the family cellar in their home and weren't bottled. In 2005 this all changed as Jaume and his wife, Toni Freixes built the new cellar down in the middle of the vines, alongside what were old farming structures that include an old olive oil mill, itself repurposed from originally being a kiln for making bricks. All of this, including a very unique old, oval well that's 22m deep are part of the tour that Jaume shows visitors.

The 40,000 bottles they produce each year are only made from their own grapes. They work to focus on grapes that are considered to be native to the region such as Carignan and Grenache, although they have minor amounts of French varietals such as Merlot, Cabernet Sauvignon, and Syrah along with some very rare, nearly extinct Catalan grapes such as Puntxó Fort. In addition to the wines, they also produce their own olive oil from the arbequina olives which is of very high quality.

🟡 **Parrell Blanc 2013**
Floral with notes of rose petals and sweet fruits in the nose. Light and subtle on the palate, it finishes with lingering floral notes.
100% Muscat

13.5% | 5€

🔴 **Parrell Jove 2013**
Aromas of dried earth, strawberries, cherry, and watermelon. Light and fresh in the body, it's also a touch dry, leading in to a short finish.
40% Grenache, 20% Syrah, 20% Merlot, 20% Cab Sauvignon

14% | 5€

🔴 **Parrell Negre**
Red fruits and sweet spices along with black pepper and a touch of graphite to the nose. The body is well balanced with a fresh acidity and medium volume with a long finish that carries notes of licorice.
40% Grenache, 20% Syrah, 20% Merlot, 20% Cab Sauvignon

14% | 5€

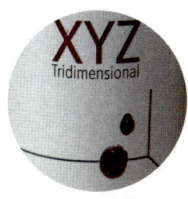

🔴 **XYZ Tridimensional 2012**
Aromas of chocolate, plums, black olives, and strawberries sitting on a bed of toasted notes. The body is dry and of decent volume overall, but doesn't have any thoroughly defined characteristics. This leads in to a finish that's a bit tannic.
60% Grenache, 20% Syrah, 20% Merlot

14% | 7€

🔴 **Parrell Roure 2011**
Dark fruits in the nose with a mix of blackberries and cherries along with touches of minerality and roses. The body is relatively light and full of the dark fruit notes. The finish has toasted notes with touches of cocoa and lingering dark fruits.
40% Grenache, 20% Syrah, 20% Merlot, 20% Cab Sauvignon

14% | 9€

Alfredo Arribas
owner

GPS
41.144681
0.810976

Alfredo Arribas
Falset, *Les Sort dels Capellans, 5*

Visits: Call or email ahead to schedule a visit and tasting.
Contact: 932531760 | alfredoarribas@portaldelpriorat.com
Website: www.portaldelpriorat.com
Languages: English and with prior notice, French and Italian

Alfredo Arribas is an architect from Barcelona who is quite renowned in Spain and internationally. With countless buildings and publications to his name, in 2001 he took something of an unexpected tangent from his main career and decided to start making wine in the Priorat region. Alfredo considers the DO Montsant and DOQ Priorat appellations as two inseparable sides of the same coin, so he wanted to make wines in both. Although his grandfather had been growing vines in the Ribera de Duero region, he says he came to Priorat with an open mind "free of the ties of tradition" that has allowed him to simply make the wines that the land suggests he makes.

In 2003 he started what was originally called, Portal del Montsant in the village of Marçà. Several of the current enological stars of DOQ Priorat started there with him and worked to build up the name, making wines that garnered a great deal of well-deserved attention. In 2007, he sold the Portal del Montsant endeavor to the Parxet winery group from Penedès and started anew in a space in Falset, but with a similar trajectory.

Afredo, now with the technical support of acclaimed enolog, Joan Asens is working to create a different style of wine that looks towards the future. Overall their wines are fresh on the palate, far less concentrated than what one is used to, but extremely nuanced and absolutely in need of tasting. All told, with the various other projects such as the Ediciones I-Limitadas and Siuralta he's producing about 50,000 bottles a year now.

🟡 **Trossos Sants 2012**
Smoky notes in the nose along with a kick of dryness. While generally controlled, the body isn't overly strong and is largely dominated by oak notes that also carry in to the finish a great deal.
100% White Grenache
13.5% | 16€

🟡 **Trossos Tros Blanc 2011**
Delicate vanilla notes to the nose as well as a hint of toast. Large and thick on the palate, it is excellent in the mouth ending in a slightly smoky finish.
100% White Grenache
14% | 41€

🔴 **Gotes del Montsant 2012**
Mix of forest fruits over a base of toasted aromas in the nose. The body is rather fresh, forthright, and strong leading in to a dry finish with lingering red fruit notes.
Grenache, Carignan
14% | 14€

🔴 **Trossos Vells 2011**
Full of mature red fruits in the nose. Aromas of a lilac and violets are blended with sweet spices such as nutmeg and notes of licorice. The body is elegant and large while remaining fresh with a perfect balance of tannins and a finish that is long and delicate with the sweet spice elements returning at the end.
100% Carignan
14% | 18€

🔴 **Trossos Tros Negre 2011**
Intense dark fruits, licorice, eucalyptus, and menthol along with herbs such as rosemary and sage in the nose. The body is voluminous, full, and potent with a long, fresh finish that boasts notes of minerality.
100% Grenache
14% | 41€

ALFREDO ARRIBAS

Gobe was one of the younger residents of Priorat who died in an unfortunate accident in 2004 in his early 20's. As he was one of the workers at Celler de Capçanes, he was naturally friends with many of the winemakers in the DO Montsant and DOQ Priorat regions and his death was a shock. As life has never been easy for rural Catalans, they are not ones to drown in a pit of sorrows after a sad event and his childhood friends came up with the idea to make a wine in Gobe's memory.

It started with a small patch of Carignan vineyards planted by Gobe's grandfather in Marçà and to which this group of 12 friends planted more vines of Grenache which totals a little over a hectare now. The production shifts a great deal from year to year, but is generally between 500-1,800 bottles of the one red wine they produce. Everyone volunteers their time on it with the enology being done at a cellar in Falset. Any money made from sales of the wine allows them to have a dinner in Gobe's honor each year and reinvest it in the project to ensure it continues to keep Gobe's memory alive while celebrating their enduring friendship.

Josep Barceló Pique
"Gobe"

GPS
41.128910
0.809712

Amics del Gobe
Marçà/Falset

Visits: N/A
Contact: 663858677 | comercial@amicsdelgobe.com
Website: www.facebook.com/AmicsDelGobe
Languages: English

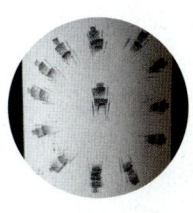

🔴 **Amics del Gobe 2011**
Sees 18 months of aging. The nose opens with aromas of plum and dark fruits that all transfer in to the body. It's a touch sweet across the palate and this aspect carries in to the finish to complete a well balanced wine.
90% Carignan, 10% Grenache

13.5% | 11€

Enric Anguera
owner

GPS
41.097729
0.702996

Anguera Domènech

Darmós, *Carrer de Sant Pere*

Visits: N/A
Contact: 977405857,654382633 | angueradomenech@gmail.com
Website: www.vianguera.com

When asking owner, Enric Anguera how long his family has been making wine, he gives that typical shrug of so many in DO Montsant which is a shorthand way to say: for generations. Naturally, this was more of a familial activity in the past and they were making the wines in the old family home. As it did for others in the region, this changed just a few years ago with the creation of the DO and Enric and his wife, Gloria Domènech looked to take the family winemaking to the next level.

They started with shifting production from the home cellar to another cellar in the village that's about 50 years old and has large underground tanks for wine production. Unlike what is typically done, Enric didn't run at these tanks with a hammer and convert them in to barrel-aging rooms. Instead, he still makes use of them to produce his wines with an annual production of around 10,000 bottles.

Currently, Enric works about 12ha of vineyards which are located just over the hill from the village. There, they have excellent exposure to the sun and cleansing breezes that come up from the Ebre River. While primarily Grenache and Carignan, they have smaller degrees of Mourvèdre, Tempranillo, Merlot, and Syrah. Most all of the vines are at least 20 years old and the Carignan lays claim to more than 50 years.

One of the loyal winery hounds

🔴 Rosat 2013
Aromas of cherries, plum, and a touch of orange peel. In the body it is light and fresh with good acidity and red fruits that become more apparent in the finish.

Grenache, Carignan, Merlot

14.5% | 5€

🔴 Reclot 2013
Red fruits, mild citrus, and spices in the nose. Light and fresh, it keeps its tannins in check while being overall balanced and leading in to a short finish that's slightly bitter with lingering spiciness.

Tempranillo, Mourvèdre, Grenache

14% | 5€

🔴 Vinya Gasó 2010
Starts out with a rather closed set of aromas to the nose and a similar character to the body. As it breathes, it opens up a bit more to express some red fruits and minor chocolate notes, but stays generally closed and reserved overall.

Grenache, Tempranillo, Carignan

13.5% | 11€

Xavier Canals
owner & enolog

GPS
41.26361
0.904022

Baronia del Montsant
Cornudella de Montsant, *Carrer de Comte de Rius, 1*

Visits: Their tasting bar and shop are open every day. They offer different types of visits and packages with restaurants in the area offering tasting menus paired with their wines. Their most typical visit includes a trip to the vineyards in a 4x4, a full tour of the cellar, and direct barrel tastings as well as tasting six of their bottled wines at a cost of 14€ per person. Call or email ahead to book a time or arrange additional options.
Contact: 977821483,667666067 | laura@baronia-m.com
Website: www.baronia-m.com
Languages: English, French

Passing through Cornudella, there is a triangular wedge of buildings where the main street of town meets the main road that passes through the village. Here, generally with their doors wide open is where Baronia del Montsant has their very easy to find cellar and tasting room.

It was started in 1998 by owner and enologist Xavier Canals, who wanted to make wines that showcased Cornudella. The high altitude vineyards they've purchased over the years and the others that they buy grapes from offer a unique style of grapes in DO Montsant. While not llicorella slate like in neighboring DOQ Priorat, the pebbly soil of their old vineyards is quite poor and doesn't hold the rain thus making for hardy grapevines that deliver deeply flavorful grapes.

Due to the geography around Cornudella there are no end of microclimates that affect each vineyard a bit differently such as an 80 year-old Grenache vineyard that exists in an air pocket formed by the Siurana reservoir. Or, others that see constant winds from the sharp face of the Montsant bluffs ducting the air upwards and out of the valley.

They work to capture all these different aspects of the locale that surrounds them by offering a large selection of different wine with different characters. Some 95% of it they export out of the country though, primarily to the US. The rest one can only assume they sell directly as the ease of visiting their tasting room makes for a popular stop on the way to see Siurana or go (or most likely come from) rock climbing.

Clos d'Englora Blanc 2012
Smoky in the nose with a pronounced nuttiness and floral notes of weaver's broom. Fat and plush in the mouth it finishes with notes of mature white fruits and nutty aspects.
100% White Grenache
13.5% | 20€

🔴 Flor d'Englora Garnatxa 2012
Dark fruits in the nose with some notes of red licorice. The body starts out on the palate discreetly but falls off sharply in the finish to be rather tannic.
100% Grenache
13.5% | 8€

🔴 Còdols del Montsant 2012
Red fruits in the nose with touches of oak. Light in the body and easy to drink, it ends in a slightly bitter finish.
100% Grenache
13.5% | 8€

🔴 Flor d'Englora Roure 2011
Fragrant in the nose with touches of violet and smokiness. The body is light in the mouth and clean leading in to a light finish that is very light.
Grenache, Carignan
13.5% | 10€

🔴 Cims del Montsant 2011
Red fruits to the nose that verge on being a bit green. Light in the body and not terribly deep but easy to drink with a short finish.
Grenache, Carignan
13.5% | 10€

🔴 Clos d'Englora AV 14 2009
Aromas of mature red fruits in the nose as well as allspice, black pepper, and oak touches. The body is quite potent with velvet tannins that lead in to a long, pleasing finish.
Grenache, Carignan, Merlot, Cab Sauvignon, Tempranillo, Cab Franc, Mourvèdre
14% | 25€

🟠 Dolç d'Englora 2009 ✦
An elaborate nose of dried plums, raisins, orange peel, hazelnuts, and cloves. Perfectly balanced in the body, holding the sweetness in check with acidity. A long, fresh finish with orange notes coming back at the end.
Grenache, Carignan
15.5% | 19.50€

In 1996, Falset native, Xavier Buil i Giné decided to start making his own wines in the DOQ Priorat. In 2005 he built his Priorat winery with the help of an investor. For their DO Montsant wines, they produce them in a rented space within DO Montsant, but they hold all their tastings and visits in the Gratallops location in DOQ Priorat.

All their wines are available to buy in their large tasting room where they welcome visitors and sell products such as the gourmet Priorat Natur line that includes vermouth, olive oil, marmalades, nuts, and other tasty products. Additionally, they have a large banquet room on the top floor for events and an exhibition hall with courses on wine tasting. As of 2013 they now also have apartments to rent at the winery with a view out over Priorat.

🟡 **Baboix Blanc 2012**
Orange peel, notes of fennel, honey, and quince in the nose. The body carries the fruit aspects well, is aromatic and leads in to a light, fresh finish.
White Grenache, Macabeu
13.5% | 11.50€

Xavier Buil i Giné
owner

GPS
41.2052
0.774267

Buil & Giné
Gratallops, *Carretera Gratallops a Vilella Baixa, km 1.5*

Visits: Drop-in tastings are possible at the shop from Monday to Sunday. The cost is 10€ for a visit and tasting of three wines and 35€ for a more detailed visit with owner.
Contact: 977839810 | info@builgine.com
Website: www.builgine.com
Languages: English, French, German

● 17·XI 2011
Smoky in the nose with subtle red fruit notes and cloves. The body is potent and markedly acidic with the barrel aspects taking center stage in the finish.
Grenache, Carignan, Tempranillo
14.5% | 9€

● Baboix 2009
Red fruits, black pepper and bell pepper to the nose. The body is a bit dry overall with a mix of acidity and herbaceous elements that are generally agreeable. The finish lingers with coffee and herbal notes.
Grenache, Carignan, Merlot, Tempranillo, Cab Sauvignon
14.5% | 17€

In the center of Darmós there is a large, imposing building from 1906 that gives little indication from the outside as to what lies within. Once you step through the doors, you're presented with a century old cellar with old, irregular tree trunks for roof beams called, "cairats" in Catalan and from which the new, Celler Cairats takes its name.

Started three years ago by Eulàlia Valls Cabré, the winery had its first vintage in 2012. They do their wine production on the main floor in the large open space that still has some of the old equipment as well as bullet marks from the Spanish Civil War. Below this are the old gigantic tanks of several thousand liters that the previous winery was making use of. Slowly they're converting them in to rooms for both barrel aging as well as hosting visitors.

Going forward and expanding upon what is now an 8,000 bottle a year production they will release a criança, aged wine as well. They want to keep things small and are working with older vines in the area to make wines they feel express the character of their region.

Eulàlia Valls Cabré
owner

GPS
41.097956
0.703661

Cairats
Darmós, *Carrer de l'Era 4-16*

Visits: Call or email ahead to schedule a visit and tasting, preferably on weekends.
Contact: 685194744,685194745 | mava.societat@gmail.com
Languages: English, French

🔴 **Carener 2012**
Slight notes of leather and vanilla in the nose as well as raspberry and dark chocolate. It's balanced in the body with small notes of spice and cocoa. Lightly dry in the finish it lingers with red fruits and chocolate.
Carignan, Merlot
14.5% | 8-9€

Núria López Sarroca
enolog & manager

GPS
41.158948
0.701314

Can Blau
El Molar, *Carretera Masroig-Molar, Km 9*

Visits: N/A
Contact: 968435022 | info@gilfamily.es
Website: www.gilfamily.es

The name Can Blau is often well known to wine lovers outside of Spain, especially in the United States. With a production of 400,000 bottles a year of which 70% is exported, their brand is easy to find far and wide. This winery is one part of group of wineries that is owned by the Gil Family. They started producing their DO Montsant wines in 2004 and in the past decade have managed to grow at a very impressive rate with their wines made from only Carignan, Grenache, and Syrah grapes.

In Catalan, "can blau" translates roughly as "blue house" and they pick up on this theme with their labels, but there actually is no house and in reality they started by using the cooperative of El Masroig with current enolog, Nuria López Sarroca joining in 2005. Their 2013 harvest was exciting for them as it was the first to be made in their brand new, enormous cellar that sits just to the south of the village of El Molar. Nuria has enjoyed the move as it allows proper space for all of their stainless steel tanks and many barrels which is very important given that each of the three wines they produce spend time in the barrels, ranging from four months to at least 20 for their top end wine.

As they settle in to the new facility they have a few more additions planned for it such as an onsite tasting room for visiting business partners as well as other facilities. It will be an impressive setting to conduct their affairs as the view from the top looks out over a wide horizon of the Priorat comarca and even a bit beyond.

🔴 Blau 2012 ⚖
Mature dark fruits in the nose with lilac and violet notes along with licorice, cumin, and orange peel. The body is balanced with dry tannins that lead in to a short finish with a minor aftertaste of the fruits found in the nose.
Carignan, Grenache, Syrah

14% | 6-7€

🔴 Can Blau 2012
Full of dark fruit aromas of blackberries and blueberries as well as notes of tobacco and cocoa that lead in to a deep, complex finish that lingers with pleasing notes of the barrels.
40% Carignan, 40% Syrah, 20% Grenache

14% | 14€

🔴 Mas de Can Blau 2010 ✴
Elegant and fragrant with a great balance of sweet fruits in the nose. The balance is carried and wonderfully maintained in the body as well as in the finish with a touch of forest fruits at the very end. A big, bold wine that is at the same time expertly crafted.
35% Carignan, 35% Syrah, 30% Grenache

15% | 35€

Francesc Capafons
owner

GPS
41.154283
0.802613

Capafons-Ossó

Falset, *Camí vell de Gratallops, Masia Esplandes*

Visits: Available by appointment at a cost of 25€ per person and include a lengthy, in-depth tour of the vineyards, and tasting of their wines. Budget a solid half a day as the experience is quite immersive and personal. English tours are available via tour guide Rachel Ritchie.
Leave the Car: For those who wish to arrive by train, the winery owners can pick you up from the Falset-Marçà station with prior notice.
Contact: 977831201, 626335785 | cellers@capafons-osso.com
Website: www.capafons-osso.cat
Languages: English

From the moment you first meet Francesc Capafons and hear him talk about Priorat, you notice that something is different. He and his wife, Montserrat Ossó are locals to Falset and you can immediately see it. Francesc can not only point out every stone and herb, but even the different subtypes. It's not a surprise, though, as Francesc and Montserrat's marriage brought together five generations of winemaking history in the area and naturally, their son, Francesc Xavier has picked up the reigns to head up the enology work in the cellar these days. After years of growing grapes and selling them to the local cooperative, they made their first vintage in 1991 and now make nearly a dozen wines in both DO Montsant and DOQ Priorat as their vineyards are split between the two.

When driving over one part of their property it becomes readily apparent that in addition to planting new vines that respect the forest and the mountains, they've also worked a great deal to recuperate the old ones that were already there. They know where they're from and they want that to show in the wines that they produce by letting the locale come through powerfully, so they farm organically and use only natural yeasts. You can see their organic production easily up in the vineyards where all manner of plants and herbs are growing amongst the vines each with a healthy respect for one another.

Their tasting room

🔴 Roigenc 2012
Wild blueberries and cherries in the nose. It's a bit hot and potent in the body and drifts towards an alcoholic, dry finish.
100% Syrah
15.1% | 10€

🟢 Auseta 2011
The nose has hints of lemon peel and slightly bitter citrus. The body is fresh and bright in the mouth and the acidity lingers in to the finish with a surprisingly degree of volume despite being a white.
100% White Grenache
14.7% | 15-17€

🔴 Vessants Xic 2010
Notes of leather, forest floor and dark fruits to the nose. The body is neutral and of medium intensity with the finish a bit tannic and dry.
37% Grenache, 36% Syrah, 27% Cab Sauvignon
14% | 10.50-12€

🔴 Vessants 2008 ⚖️
A warm, rich nose full of caramel and toffee elements. The body switches up a good deal and kicks up the acidity and dark fruits. It pulls out in to a relatively fresh finish that carries the acidity a touch.
30% Grenache, 20% Carignan, 20% Cab Sauvignon, 10% Syrah, 10% Merlot
15% | 10.50-12€

🔴 Masia Esplanes 2005
A mix of slightly earthy aromas mixed in with stronger minerality in the nose and a dose of dark cherry elements when first opened. The minerality holds steady in the body, kicks up a touch of acidity, but keeps it quite nicely balanced and light across the palate. The finish is dry and brings up the tannins a bit while-leaving a dusting of dried figs in the mouth.
40% Merlot, 35% Cab Sauvignon, 15% Syrah, 10% Grenache
14.5% | 16-18€

Àngel Teixidó
enolog

GPS
41.101598
0.781037

Celler de Capçanes
Capçanes, *Carrer de Llaberia, 4*

Visits: Their shop at the cellar is open daily. Call or email ahead for a full visit that includes a taste of three wines for a price of 8€.
Leave the Car: The cellar is located immediately next to the Capçanes train station.
Contact: 977178319 | cellercapcanes@cellercapcanes.com
Website: www.cellercapcanes.com
Languages: English, French

The fact that Capçanes is serious about wine is no better shown than when entering the village and there, immediately on the left, is the big winery ready to greet you. Life focuses a great deal around the cellar with it having 80 associates, many of whom live in the 400 person village. Then of course there are others who work at the cellar as well.

The foundation of this cooperative dates from 1933 when five families in the village joined together to form a more efficient and marketable union. By sharing equipment and production they were able to greatly lower the costs of their wines and better compete in the market.

Their production continued in this manner for decades, selling their wine in bulk until 1995 brought about a serious change to the direction of the winery. The Jewish community of Barcelona inquired about their ability to produce a Kosher wine. They agreed to work on this and essentially created a cellar within the main cellar to keep the Kosher wine separate from the general production and touched only by the Rabbi making it.

Now, they currently produce about 650,000 bottles a year along with 250,000 liters of bulk and bag-in-box wines. All of their grapes come from the nearby villages of Capçanes, Els Guiamets, Marçà, Tivissa, and Falset making them a true cellar of southern DO Montsant.

🟢 **2/vb 2009**
A blanc de noir, the nose has a cream aspect to it which, while holds aromas of white fruits. The body is incredibly fresh and mineral with notes of mint and strawberry. The finish is also fresh with a lingering note of raspberry. A fascinating take on this method.
100% Grenache
15% | 27.50€

🔴 Mas Donis Barrica 2012
Strong red fruit aromas along with strawberries and fennel. The body holds good acidity and is overall pleasing, leading in to a quick, easy to drink finish.

85% Grenache, 15% Syrah

14% | 6€

🔴 Costers del Gravet 2010
Red fruit notes in the nose along with a clean freshness to it. Light and discreet in the mouth it carries the fresh aspects in to a finish that's a touch tannic.

Cab Sauvignon, Grenache, Carignan

14.5% | 13.50€

🔴 Peraj Ha'abib 2012 ★
Intense aromas of red and dark fruits as well as cedar notes and touches of vanilla and black pepper. The body has an excellent initial attack with good acidity and bold fruit flavors as well as herbs and spices. The finish lingers but sticks a bit much on the palate.

Grenache, Carignan

14.5% | 26€

🔴 Cabrida 2010
Aromas of mature plums as well as coffee, chocolate, and orange peel. The body is elegant with mature, evolved tannins and a touch velvety. The finish is long and pleasing with a touch of sweetness at the end.

100% Grenache

15% | 40€

🟠 Pansal del Calàs 2010
Aromas of dried figs and preserved oranges. Large and round in the body, it's very fresh overall with floral notes that hold strong in to the finish. A good companion for dark chocolate.

Grenache, Carignan

16% | 20€

CELLER DE CAPÇANES

Cara Nord is a cellar project by three people who have worked in wine for a long time: Tomàs Cusiné who has a winery in neighboring DO Costers del Segre, winery manager Xavier Cepero, and US distributor Eric Solomon. They wanted to make wines from vineyards of high altitude and thus, Cara Nord or "north face of a mountain" was born in March of 2012.

While the wines that are perhaps more well-known from the project are the red and white they produce from vineyards in Muntanyes de Prades under DO Conca de Barberà they also recently started producing this one DO Montsant wine. Made from grapes found in the upper reaches of the region, it makes for a fresh and unique take on a mostly Carignan wine.

Cara Nord
La Bisbal del Falset

Visits: N/A
Contact: 973176029 | hola@caranordceller.com
Website: www.caranordceller.com
Languages: English

🔴 **Mineral del Montsant 2012**
Wonderful bouquet of forest fruits and minerality as well as spices such as cardamom. The body is large and smooth in the mouth with a fantastic mix of spices that all slide in to a lingering finish and a wine that maintains great freshness overall.
80% Carignan, 20% Grenache

14% | 10€

Xavi Cedó
enolog & owner

GPS
41.081494
0.739902

Cedó Anguera
La Serra d'Almos, *Carretera de La Serra d'Almos*

Visits: Weekends are preferred, but other times can be scheduled all with calling ahead to make an appointment. Visits are currently free.
Contact: 699694728 | celler@cedoanguera.com
Website: www.cedoanguera.com
Languages: English

When entering the rather remote village of La Serra d'Almos, off on the right it's impossible to miss the winery of Cedó Anguera. The large yellow building sits atop long rows of vineyards. These however are but a small part of the total 18ha that they grow. It's a considerable production for a family winery and this mix of 60% Carignan, 30% Grenache, along with a little Syrah, and Cabernet Sauvingon, is by and large sold off to other cellars in the DO.

Prior to the formation of DO Montsant, they, like most of the other wineries in the area, were selling off all the grapes they grew, primarily to the cooperative located in La Serra d'Almos. But, in 2006 they decided to build their current cellar which Xavi Cedó has been running since their first vintage in 2007. Amazingly, all of their 18ha of vineyards are within the village borders and despite the amount they sell, they also produce 40-45,000 bottles a year. All of the vinification is made in stainless steel tanks for the young wines or larger, 300L barrels for the aged wines.

As is the case with many of the family cellars, they also grow olives which they press at the local cooperative who produce one of the most fantastic oils found in the region.

Their barrel room

🟤 Anexe 2012
Mature plums to the nose as well as earthy chocolate notes. The body is of medium strength and a touch sweet and buttery. The finish recalls the fruit elements and lingers nicely.

Carignan, Grenache, Syrah

13.5% | 5€

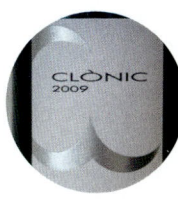

🟤 Clònic 2009
A mix of red and dark fruits in the nose as well as balsamic and forest floor touches. The body is light and has a strong toasted character. The finish is a touch bitter with cocoa notes at the end.

Carignan, Cab Sauvignon, Syrah

14% | 9€

🟤 Clònic Vinyes Velles de Samsó 2012
Very mature red fruits to the nose along with a strong floral component. The body has good minerality and a touch of black pepper. The finish is a bit astringent with downplayed fruits.

100% Carignan

14.5% | 12€

CEDÓ ANGUERA

Magí Baiget
manager

GPS
41.231285
0.901047

Cingles Blaus
Cornudella de Montsant, *Mas de les Moreres*

Visits: N/A
Contact: 977326080,657969185 | cinglesblaus@cinglesb-laus.com
Website: www.cinglesblaus.com

Before reaching the almighty Priorat landmark of La Venta del Pubill, there is a dirt road off to the right which, when followed for about a half a kilometer you come to what looks like a small village. This cute little settlement of 15th century stone homes is Mas de les Moreres and two cellars have been established here, Celler de d'Era and Cingles Blaus.

Owned by the Busquet family, Cingles Blaus started making their wines initially at the cooperative of Cornudella in 2001. They moved to the Mas de les Moreres property in 2005 to produce all of their wines in the cellar that they built in one of the old buildings. Currently they produce upwards of 40,000 bottles a year.

To meet this production, in total they now own 8ha of vineyards that are situated around the masia and they buy some from the high altitude vineyards near Cornudella. They find themselves selling most of the production locally in Catalonia as opposed to exporting.

The front of the old cellar

🔴 Octubre Rosat 2012
Has an aromatic intensity to it with strawberry, roses, and light herbal notes to the nose. Fresh and direct in the body it departs in the finish with a well-defined acidity and surprising depth.
60% Grenache, 40% Carignan
13.5% | 6€

🟢 Octubre Blanc 2011
Aromas of green apple, pear, and white flowers. Fresh in the body it stays light and fresh in to the finish.
White Grenache, Macabeu
12.5% | 6€

🔴 Octubre Negre 2011
Red fruits along with yogurt and menthol in the nose. The body has an astringent element to it that keeps it rather closed and leads in to a simple, easy to enjoy finish.
60% Grenache, 40% Carignan
13.5% | 7-8€

🔴 Mas de les Moreres 2009
Complex assortment of aromas including graphite, thyme, dark forest fruits, and a little leather. Very well structured with large tannins from the oak that then carry in to the finish.
Cab Sauvignon, Carignan, Grenache, Merlot, Syrah
14% | 11€

Maruxa Roel
enolog & manager

GPS
41.139898
0.784489

Clos Pissarra

Falset, *Carretera Falset-Móra la Nova, Km 7*

Visits: N/A
Contact: 626656730 | maruxa.roel@gmail.com
Website: www.miuravineyards.com

Clos Pissarra is a curious creation. While the cellar and all of its vineyards are certified within DO Montsant and they produce seven different wines, not a single one of them has DO certification and the labels are only in English. The reason behind this for this is that they export 99% of their 75,000 bottles to the US and Puerto Rico with just a few being sold locally in a handful of stores.

How this winery came to be is that it is one cellar within the portfolio of a company called Miura that owns three different wineries in California, Catalonia, and Southern France. While there are several owners behind the company, one of the main ones who was behind the push to create this cellar in the Priorat comarca was Emmanuel Kemiji. The 12th American to pass the Master Sommelier exam in London, he's worked extensively as the wine director at prominent restaurants in California including the The Dining Room at the Ritz-Carlton in San Francisco.

With native Galician, Maruxa Roel heading up the enology and management of the cellar, they created this winery in 2003 and purchased the 17ha of land around the cellar where they planted new vineyards of Grenache, Carignan, Cabernet Sauvignon, Merlot, and Syrah. Despite the fact that their trajectory is fully for the export market, they work to create wines that express the region as much as anyone else and the cellar is a fully gravity-fed operation.

One part of their vineyards

🟡 El Sol Blanc 2011
Apricot, chalk, acacia flowers, mature pears, and a touch of lactic aromas to the nose. The body expresses a large acidity that would make for good pairing with bold dishes. The finish lingers with mature fruits.
100% White Grenache

14%

🔴 Arrels 2012
A discreet nose with dark fruits, mature quince, and small vegetal notes. The body is light and slightly sweet in the mouth with a full texture. The finish is clean, fresh, and makes for an easy to drink wine.
100% Grenache

14%

🔴 Aristan 2012
Aromas of jammy, mature cherries, along with forest fruits and quince. The body departs a great deal from the nose being dry and young, leading in to a similar finish with mature red fruits lingering.
Grenache, Syrah

14%

🔴 El Ramon 2009 ✶
Dark fruits, graphite, balsamic, and rich notes of toffee to the nose. Very full and spicy in the mouth, yet still balanced, it leads in to a lingering finish with notes of plum and forest fruits.
Grenache, Carignan, Cab Sauvignon

14% | 17€

CLOS PISSARRA

Toni & Miquel Coca i Fitó
owners

GPS
41.12452
0.734447

Coca i Fitó
El Masroig, *Avinguda Onze de Septembre*

Visits: Call or email ahead to have a tasting and cellar visit for up to 10 people at a cost of 10€ per person.
Contact: 665220796 | info@cocafito.com
Website: www.cocafito.com
Languages: English

Growing up in the Catalan wine heartland of Alt Penedès, it's amazing to find out that brothers Toni and Miquel Coca i Fitó don't have a family history of making wine. This amazement is due to Miquel successfully exporting a great swath of Catalan wines and Toni being a superstar consulting enolog for over a dozen quality wineries in Catalonia. But Coca i Fitó is their personal baby where they're given free rein to make, design, and sell the wines exactly as they want and do so quite successfully.

The urge to start their own winery came about after Toni had worked at many wineries in the Priorat comarca and found himself in love with the wine that could be produced in both DOQ Priorat and DO Montsant. While they produce a very impressive 160,000 bottles a year now, it started out considerably smaller back in 2006 when they made their first vintage at the Sant Rafel winery in Pradell de la Teixeta which Toni still consults for.

In 2011 they made the move to El Masroig as they found themselves growing quickly and in need of a new, large space for production. Their current cellar used to be an old winery with large deposits for bulk wine production in the floor. They've since converted these in to separate rooms where they store their mix of 7-8 different types of barrels. This is a crucial aspect of their production given that they age the grapes from all the vineyards they harvest from separately prior to blending.

As to the future, they continue to grow and collaborate with other wineries, such as their joint project with Roig Parals from DO Empordà to make the "Tocat" line of wines. Soon though, they'll probably have to move again to an even bigger cellar to house what has become their new family winery in Montsant.

🔴 **Coca i Fitó Rosa 2012**
Aromas of strawberries, cherries, plums, and currants in the nose. The body, while being a Rosé has the soul of a red wine and is very fresh leading in to a finish with red fruit notes.
100% Syrah
14% | 11€

🔴 **Jaspi Negre 2011**
Complex mineral notes with a touch of fresh balsamic aromas in the nose. The body is full in the mouth and well balanced between fruit, oak, and alcohol. The finish is full of dark fruits and spice notes from the oak.
45% Grenache, 25% Carignàn, 15% Cab Sauvignon, 15% Syrah
14.5% | 8.50€

🔴 **Jaspi Maragda 2010**
Full of red fruit aromas and a touch of butter to the nose. The body is meaty and fresh leading in to a slightly bitter, but buttery and rich finish.
55% Grenache, 25% Carignan, 20% Syrah
14.5% | 13.50€

🔴 **Coca i Fitó Negre 2009**
Notes of minerals, violets, cocoa, toffee, caramel, and balsamic aromas. The body is round, velvety, and very well constructed, leading in to a long, elegant and well balanced finish.
50% Syrah, 30% Grenache, 20% Carignan
14.5% | 24€

🟠 **Dolç**
Red fruit comfit in the nose with light, young plum aromas. Rich and balanced in the mouth with good acidity and freshness. Dried figs in the finish.
Grenache, Carignan
15.5% | 20€

Pep Aguilar & Patri Morillo
owners & enologs

GPS
41.149054
0.829749

Comunica
Falset, *Finca Fontanals*

Visits: N/A
Contact: 600753840,607531018 | yalellamaremos@yahoo.es
Languages: English

If you spend any time visiting wineries in Catalonia, then chances are that you'll probably drink at least one wine that's been touched at some point by Pep Aguilar and Patri Morillo, the two enologs who own Comunica. If you get the chance to meet them, you'll also quickly realize that by most people's definitions, they're completely insane. A typical day for them is comprised of consulting for one of several cellars they contract with all over Catalonia. Then they either work on their Comunica project in Falset or the very unique Biu project way, way up in Pyrenees. Given that they live on the coast of Catalonia, they are pretty much always in the car on their way to some kind of wine adventure. But when you catch them, they always seem to somehow make time to share their wines with a nice friendly chat as wines are meant to be drank.

Their longstanding partnership started years ago when they met each other on a commuter train while studying at the university. Eventually they found themselves to be roommates with other students, sharing a flat with a couple of other girls. One of which Patri ended up marrying and another ended up being enolog Anna Espelt who directs her family's very successful winery up in Empordà now.

Finishing their studies they began to work for a long list of cellars and eventually they formed their enology consultancy fittingly called, "ya le llamaremos" which in Castilian means, "we'll call you". Eventually they formed a plan to create their own wine label in DO Montsant and call it "Comunica" to keep with the theme that they're always on the phone and well, communicating whether via the bottle or the phone. This project started in 2010 with the winemaking taking place at the cellar of Pascona.

While they have been producing two wines under the Comunica label, working closely at Pascona allowed them to create a third wine with Toni Ripoll (the son in charge of enology for Pascona) which is called, La Comèdia. All of these wines are from grapes that range 25-30 years old and are made in a similar style wherein they work to directly express the locale, use no oak barrels, and an absolute minimum of sulfur. With these three wines they produce about 28,000 bottles a year and are quite popular given that they're very approachable both in terms of taste as well as the overall price points.

🔴 La Comedia 2012
Fresh in the nose overall and has light herbal notes mixed with black pepper, red fruits, and a hint of strawberries. The body continues with the freshness and adds touches of coffee as well as sage, fennel, and the red fruits from the nose. The herbal notes linger in to the finish with a mild acidity.
50% Grenache, 50% Carignan

13.5% | 9€

🔴 Comunica 2011
Notes of cranberry and vanilla with pleasant touches of caramel. The body is round, meaty and presents blueberries, dark chocolate and a great balance despite the wine acting like it wants to get out of control at any moment. The finish is clean, and perfect. Decanting brings out more structure and freshness.
100% Grenache

13.5% | 12-15€

🔴 Comunica Samsó 2011
Starts out with some tart citric and lactic notes along with a degrees of red fruits. These blend with the clay elements that are typical of the Carignan. With time, the aromas gain a degree of round strawberry and mature cherry aspects. The body is wonderfully balanced with bell pepper notes alongside fresh, lively acidity. These qualities all carry in to a fresh, lively finish.
100% Carignan

13.5% | 17€

GPS
41.263707
0.904408

Celler Cooperatiu de Cornudella
Cornudella de Montsant, *Carrer de Comte de Rius, 1*

Visits: They have organized visits every Saturday & Sunday at noon or with calling ahead to reserve an alternate time. The tour and taste of three wines is 10€ with a maximum of 20 people. Their shop with wines and local products is open every day.
Contact: 977821329 | info@cornudella.net
Website: www.cornudella.net

Directly facing the main road sits an architectural gem of a cellar. Classified as one of the "Wine Cathedrals", the cellar of the cooperative of Cornudella is an exquisite representation of the art nouveau style that was created in the early 20th century in Catalonia. The architect, Cèsar Martinell Brunet was a disciple of Antoni Gaudí and he is responsible for creating this, along with the cooperative in Falset and others in Catalonia such as the one in Gandesa.

Looking at the front, it's easy to see how the façade made use of the stone found locally around Cornudella and that with its central nave and small, angular windows, it was designed to emulate an actual cathedral. Started in 1919 and finished in 1921, it was the cooperative of winemakers in the village who requested its construction. Reeling from the devastation that phylloxera had brought to their livelihood, they banded together for safety and hired Martinell to build what was at the time, a very modern cellar in order to make their wines more commercially viable with their first vintage in the new cellar in 1922.

Despite the initial size of the cellar they had to build a large extension to handle additional capacity in the 1950's, although this addition was made in the same exact style. For decades they made only bulk wines, but starting in 1981 they began to produce bottled wines under DO Tarragona which then changed to DO Montsant in 2002. Now, they produce about 70,000 bottles a year of red, white, sweet, and mistela.

As this wondrous building aged, it was in need of repair and the foundation of the bank, La Caixa funded a good deal of the first stage of renovation to make sure that their building continues to stay with us. Unfortunately, the same can't be said of the cooperative members which currently count about 82 producers. They too are getting older and many are starting to retire, leaving the future of the cooperative, like many in the region, uncertain.

🔴 Les Troies 2012 ⚖

Dark fruits, stony minerality, and a touch of balsamic notes to the nose. It flirts with having decent roundness to the body and finishes with herbaceous notes.

Grenache, Carignan

13.5% | 4€

🔴 El Codolar 2011

Full of aromas of red fruits, cocoa, cherries, and strawberries. The body is fresh and light and leads in to a short, but enjoyable finish.

50% Grenache, 50% Carignan

13.5% | 5.50€

🔴 Castell del Siurana 2010

Intensely aromatic with red fruits and an undercurrent of herbaceous elements. Relatively expressive in the body, it leads in to a dry finish with an aftertaste of red fruits.

70% Grenache, 30% Carignan

13.5% | 8.50€

GPS
41.12452
0.734447

DiT
El Masroig, *Avinguda Onze de Septembre*

Visits: N/A
Contact: 619777419 | info@cocafito.com
Languages: English

When it comes to wine production a great deal of it is industrial with little care for land and a desire to only create a bottle that can sell regardless of how it was produced. Toni Coca and Dani Sánchez were very aware of this and in 2007 they joined forces to create a line of wines that were all fully organic. Having known each other for years after first meeting while working in DOQ Priorat, this was a grand undertaking with the resulting cellar being called DiT for Dani i Toni. It was the very first organic cellar in DO Montsant.

All of the wines are made at the same cellar as Coca i Fitó (Toni's other project with his brother Miquel) in the village of El Masroig. Toni is responsible for the winemaking and Dani handles the viticulture side of things as he has his own cellar in Navarra called, Azul y Garanza. They've been growing over time and are currently producing about 50,000 bottles a year.

Selenita Rosat 2012
Red fruits to the nose with a good deal of acidity present. Generally smooth and balanced in the body the finish returns to the acidic notes along with an ending perk of freshness.
60% Syrah, 40% Grenache
14% | 7.40€

🟡 Cabirol Blanc 2012
Aromas of dried apricot as well as floral notes of chamomile and thyme. The body is ample in the mouth and leads in to a lingering finish with honey notes.
65% White Grenache, 35% Macabeu
14% | 6.50€

🔴 Cabirol Negre 2011
Notes of blueberries, cured cherries, and light toffee. The body is full and buttery with a pleasing finish and mature fruit notes at the end.
60% Grenache, 20% Tempranillo
14.5% | 6.50€

🔴 Selenita 2010
Toasted aromas along with green bell pepper and spicy black pepper notes. Dry in the mouth, the body presents touches of the oak with a medium length finish.
50% Grenache, 30% Syrah, 20% Cab Sauvignon
14.5% | 9€

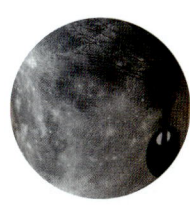

🔴 Tanit 2010
Buttery notes along with cedar, cocoa, and forest floor. The body is round and easy to drink with black fruits at the base. The finish is light and dry pulling in balsamic notes at the very end. A fine wine for hearty dishes such as oxtail.
70% Grenache, 30% Carignan
14.5% | 15€

Àngel Teixidó is the head enolog of Celler de Capçanes and knows the grapes from the region exceedingly well. He, along with Jürgen Wagner decided back in 1994 to create a Carignan wine from parcels around the village that would show how great the grape can be from all four types of soil that comprise the village lands.

The result of this effort is called, Dos Pájaros which in Castilian means, "two birds" and if you look at the label you'll indeed see two birds, each wearing traditional costumes from Jürgen's Germany and Àngel's Catalonia. Given that it's a side project they do purely to experiment with the local grapes, Àngel admits that the number of "birds" involved changes from year to year. So, while the current release is Dos Pájaros, years before were Tres or Cinco Pájaros. In the end, the focus remains the same though with about 2-4,000 bottles made each year.

Àngel Teixidó
enolog & co-owner

GPS
41.101598
0.781037

Dos Pájaros
Capçanes, *Carrer de Llaberia, 4*

Visits: N/A
Contact: a.teixido@cellercapcanes.com

● **Dos Pájaros 2010**
Aromas of light red fruits with touches of raspberry predominating as well as dried plums, carob, and slight balsamic notes. The body is more pronounced with dark fruits, spicy black pepper, and licorice that leads in to a round, plush finish with floral notes of violets.
100% Carignan
15% | 45€

Dos Terras has the distinction of being the only cellar in the region joined with a rural hotel by the name of Mas Figueres. The history of this estate dates back to the early 19th century when it was built by scientist, Juan de la Fuente to carry out experiments with a good degree of rural solitude. The overall style is reminiscent of the Spanish Colonial architecture that was popular at the time and sitting down below the road between Falset and Marçà it has served as a refuge for artists and writers throughout the years.

In 2007 enologist, Josep Grau bought the property and built the winery. He had been producing the Dos Terras wines previously though in nearby Capçanes from what started out as 3ha of vineyards spread over two different soil types, thus creating the original name of the winery. Over time they have slowly grown in production to make about 32,000 bottles a year from their vineyards that range from 40 to 100 years old and are now culled from 16ha of total vines. Enolog Noe Javierre has been overseeing the winemaking in recent vintages and at the end of 2013, Fernando Grajales bought both the winery and hotel with an eye towards changing the trajectory a bit.

Noe Javierre
enolog

GPS
41.129878
0.80839

Dos Terras
Marçà, *Mas Figueres*

Visits: Available weekends, with a previous appointment, or for guests of the masia at a cost of 5€ for a tasting and 10€ for a tasting with a visit of the vineyards.
Contact: 977178011, 627999343
Website: www.dosterras.com
Languages: English, French

● **Dos Terras 2010**
Red fruits in the nose and overall quite well balanced with balsamic notes in the body that carry in to a finish that's a touch bitter at the end. Could easily stand for another two years in the bottle.
100% Grenache
14.5% | 18€

● **Finca Aiguasals 2011**
A potent nose that expresses iron and flint aspects alongside jammy notes that make for a most intricate composition of aromas. In the body, it's elegant and wonderfully structured with a long, persistent finish.
100% Carignan
14.5% | 43€

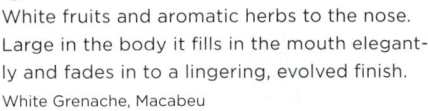

This is a project started by Alfredo Arribas that he makes at his DO Montsant cellar in Falset. Essentially he considers this to be an "editorial" of wines wherein he and his enologs work to select what they consider to be the most interesting pieces of each harvest. So, the nature of the project changes a little bit from year to year although they work to maintain the same labels.

Additionally, they create custom blends and labels for clients upon request.

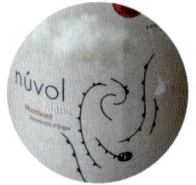

🟡 **Núvol 2012**

White fruits and aromatic herbs to the nose. Large in the body it fills in the mouth elegantly and fades in to a lingering, evolved finish.
White Grenache, Macabeu

13% | 9€

Alfredo Arribas
owner

GPS
41.144681
0.810976

Ediciones I-limitadas
Falset, *Les Sort dels Capellans, 5*

Visits: N/A
Contact: 629341231 | info@edicionesi-limitadas.com
Website: www.edicionesi-limitadas.com
Languages: English

● **Luno 2011**
Red fruits notes of strawberries, plums, and currants along with orange peel. Very agreeable in the body and easy to drink it finishes with the notes found in the nose.
Grenache, Carignan, Syrah, Cab Sauvignon
14% | 8€

● **Faunus 2012**
Touch of earthiness and a compote of apricots, cherries, and red bell pepper to the nose. Very pleasing and easygoing in the body, it finishes with a very balanced, lingering character.
Carignan, Tempranillo, Merlot, Syrah
14% | 10€

Jordi Torrella
enolog & manager

GPS
41.231594
0.901965

Celler de l'Era
Cornudella de Montsant, *Mas de les Moreres*

Visits: To visit both Celler de l'Era along with Mas d'en Blei is 10€ per person. To visit just Celler de l'Era is 6€. They can accommodate between two and 12 people.
Contact: 977262031, 686246679 | info@cellerdelera.com
Website: www.cellerdelera.com
Languages: English, French, Portuguese

Down the same road as Cingles Blaus sits Celler de l'Era. This cellar comprises what is nearly the end of Mas de les Moreres, a 15th century "micro" village of old and beautiful stone houses just outside of Cornudella. This used to be the road to Reus decades upon decades ago and it was an important stop along the way, which is one of the reasons these houses were built up and established along the banks of the Arbolí River.

The history of this winery dates back to 2002 when current owner, Albert Tasias and his family bought the property and then shortly after, planted the vines. The old home that sits in front of the cellar Albert uses as a part-time residence and he's maintained the history of it exceedingly well with their tasting room set in one of the old stone halls. The old cement tanks where they made wine in the past are preserved as well.

Their first harvest was in 2010 and currently they produce about 50,000 bottles a year released under two different labels made only from grapes harvested on the 12ha of mature vineyards they now have. Heading this up is the enologist and manager, Jordi Torrella who also runs the winery, Mas d'en Blei very nearby in DOQ Priorat. The owner of Celler de l'Era and Mas d'en Blei happen to be friends and while they maintain separate cellars for their respective wineries, Jordi and his winery team split their time and some of the equipment between the two.

They also offer joint visits and tastings that allow people to compare wines from both DOs.

🔴 **Bri 2010**

Mineral and anise aromas as well as a touch of licorice and red fruits such as strawberry and raspberry. The body is intense and mineral with well-balanced tannic notes that lead in to a long, wonderful finish.

Grenache, Carignan, Cab Sauvignon

13.5% | 12€

🔴 **Mim 2010**

Nicely balanced in the nose with notes of white pepper and dark fruits. The body has deep mineral notes along with a greater extrapolation of the fruit aromas that end with a delicate finish that sits on the palate perfectly.

Grenache, Carignan, Cab Sauvignon

14%

Their tasting room

It's very important to note that this is not a cellar, but it's included in the DO Montsant and they do produce wine. The catch is that the wine isn't for sale because it's made by the professors and students of the Falset enology school.

This school, located behind the Falset High School and across the road from research center ViTec is a very important component of winemaking for not just DO Montsant and DOQ Priorat, but Catalonia and Spain as a whole. Started in 1982 by priest Jaume Ciurana, it was created by the people of Priorat to further modernize their winemaking by having qualified enologs. Each year they have about 35 students--half from Catalonia and half from outside the region. Students learn all of the aspects of winemaking from vine cultivation to vinification to aging and a great deal more such as distillation and brewing. This two year program has provided the training for many of the enologs working at today's wineries.

Near to the school they have 1.2ha of vineyards where the students learn how to care for them as well as try various experiments in regards to pruning or watering the vines. The grapes from these vineyards are used to make the school wine each year that they've been keeping and aging.

GPS
41.154252
0.825176

Escola d'Enologia Jaume Ciurana

Falset, *Carretera de Falset-Porrera, Km 1*

Visits: N/A
Contact: 627508134, 977830338
Website: escoladenologia-inspriorat.blogspot.com

● **Criança 2009**
Aromas of rose petals, sour cherries and licorice. The body, while a bit muddled at first fleshes out well and finishes strongly offering more sour cherry notes and spice. A wine that could easily age more years.
Cab Sauvignon, Grenache, Carignan
13.5%

When looking down from the top of this vineyard and starting to descend the stone paths, the thought crosses the mind repeatedly as to why on earth anyone would make terraces so steep? But, they did and it's an incredible site to behold with its old vine Grenache clinging to the side of a windswept peak called either Aubacs or Solans depending on the sun orientation that eventually leads up to the Ermita de Sant Pau.

While the old part of the vineyard has been dutifully tended to and many vines are ungrafted and would seem to be pre-phylloxera, it was Patri of Comunica who came upon it one day and told the owner that he had something special on his hands. René Barbier, Fernando Zamora, and Christopher Cannan made the decision to rent the vineyard and in 2004 started producing the ridiculously good l'Espectacle with René handling the enology at Laurona. The name comes from when René and Christopher saw the vineyard for the first time on a clear day, being able to see to the Pyrenees, 120km away and said, "This is a spectacle". They produce between 4-5,000 bottles a year of this wine that shows just how good DO Montsant can really be. It's almost always in lists of the Top 10 wines from Catalonia.

René Barbier III
enolog & co-owner

GPS
41.219703
0.715881

L'Espectacle
La Figuera, *Camí de l'Ermita de Sant Pau*

Visits: N/A
Website: www.espectaclevins.com
Languages: English, French

🔴 **L'Espectacle 2012**
An incredible mix of aromas including forest fruits, blueberries, and graphite minerality as well as toasted hazelnuts in a luscious, full nose. Large and wonderful in the mouth, it's full and fresh leading in to a lingering, elegant finish that hangs effortlessly on the palate.
100% Grenache
15% | 110€

CELLER COOPERATIU 19

Marta Ferré
enolog

GPS
41.142794
0.818073

Ètim - Cooperativa Falset Marçà
Falset, *Carrer de Miquel Barceló, 31*

Visits: Their shop is open daily for purchases of wine, oil, and other local products. They have scheduled, "theatric" visits of the winery on weekends that are ideal for people with children and it's also possible to reserve a regular visit other times as well.
Leave the Car: The cellar is located in the center of Falset and via a quick shuttle bus or bike ride can be reached by arriving at the Marçà-Falset train station.
Contact: 977830105, 699946633 | visita@etim.cat
Website: www.la-cooperativa.cat
Languages: English

The cellar of Ètim is very hard to miss in Falset. One of the largest buildings in this small town, it is also a wonderful example of the art nouveau "Wine Cathedrals" that were built in the early 20th century. Like the cooperative in Cornudella, the architect was Cèsar Martinell Brunet, a disciple of Antoni Gaudí who was responsible for creating this, along with other cooperative cellars in Catalonia. As with the others, a local touch was added to make it unique which in this case is that it mimics elements of the Falset Castle which sits on a hill directly in front of the cellar.

This lovely "cathedral" was built in 1919, but the formation of the cooperative predates it by seven years when 350 farmers in the area joined together to form the cooperative of Falset in 1912. Naturally finding safety in numbers and also sharing wine production equipment worked to their advantage and the winery was quite successful.

They initially started with only bulk wine production, but added in bottles as well. Starting in the 1980's, membership in cooperatives throughout the region started to fall. So, in 1999, this cooperative in Falset merged with the cooperative of Marçà. They officially became the Cooperative of Falset-Marçà and make use the facilities of the Falset cellar with Portal del Montsant taking over the old Marçà space.

Walking through the cellar is impressive as the architecture of the space still looks great today due to maintenance over the years. Inside, the first thing that you see are these huge tanks that they use to make their 750,000 bottles a year. But those old wooden tanks at the front are where they make their quite wonderful vermouth. Everything is sold under the joint Ètim name which in Catalan means, "the original meaning". All told, they export their wines to over 30 countries as well as having a loyal following right at home.

🔴 **Rosat 2012**

Overall fresh in aromas and body with a strong aspect of strawberries as well as some smaller pepper notes.

100% Grenache

14.5% | 6.50€

🟡 **Blanc 2012**

Subtle notes of apricot to the nose along with almonds and an overall freshness. The body continues with this fresh aspect and leads in to a finish with floral notes and a well-defined acidity.

100% White Grenache

13.5% | 6.50€

🟡 **Castell de Falset Garnatxa Blanca 2009**

Aromas of tropical fruits, dried flowers, and mandarin. In the body it's round and well integrated with a touch of the tropical elements coming through and leading in to a long, smooth finish.

100% White Grenache

14% | 15€

🔴 **Negre 2011**

Aromas of cherries as well as dried plums. Fresh and round in the body with a well-balanced acidity although somewhat green. It has a dry, lingering finish that would allow the wine to pair well with grilled meats.

Grenache, Carignan, Syrah

14.5% | 6.50€

🔴 **Old Vines Grenache 2008**
Notes of dried plums as well as a cocoa, graphite, and a touch of vanilla to the nose. The body is large and full with red fruits notes such as mature cherries that lead in to a short finish with rather prevalent alcoholic notes.
85% Grenache, 15% Cab Sauvignon
14.5% | 10€

🔴 **Castell de Falset 2006**
Aromas of blackberries, strawberries, and touches of orange peel in the nose as well as allspice. The body is velvety and potent leading in to a strong, sweet finish.
Grenache, Carignan, Cab Sauvignon
14.5% | 15€

🔴 **Selection Syrah 2006**
Balsamic notes along with aromas of blackberries, licorice, and black pepper in the nose. The body is well structured and lingers with an elegant aspect in to the very enjoyable finish.
100% Syrah
13.5% | 19.50€

🔴 **L'Esparver 2006**
Dark chocolate notes in the nose along with blackberries and touches of orange as well as a dried plums. After a body that is dry in texture, the aromatic elements return to the finish.
100% Grenache
14% | 25€

🟠 **Tradition Verema Tardana Blanc 2011**
Quince and orange peel aromas as well as a distinct petrol quality to the nose. The body is full and sweet across the palate. A hint of the nose comes in to the play in the finish as well as a lingering dryness.
100% White Grenache
14% | 8.50€

🟠 **Tradition Verema Tardana Negre 2011**
Intense with dark fruits in the nose giving off aromas of plums, figs, and cherry as well as a touch of chocolate. It fills in the palate wonderfully and finishes with long, lingering tastes of nuts and orange peel.
100% Grenache
15% | 8.50€

🟠 **Ranci**
Lovely oxidized notes of dried fruits and nuts while staying light on the palate and drifting in to elegant, caramel flavors that appear in the finish.
Grenache, Carignan
17% | 8€

Jaume Roca
co-owner

GPS
41.216122
0.732036

Ficaria Vins
La Figuera, *Carrer del Priorat, 12*

Visits: Call or email ahead for a reservation. The cost is 8€ per person for a taste and a visit to the cellar. For a taste, cellar visit, and vineyard visit the cost is 12€ per person.
Contact: 617548453 | celler@ficariavins.net
Website: www.ficariavins.net
Languages: English (with notice), French

Jaume Roca and his wife Montse Castro have a strong sense of village pride. They're both from La Figuera, the remote, high altitude yet picturesque village on the west side of the Priorat comarca. Lovers of wine, they've known (as have other DO Montsant cellars) that the Grenache grown in La Figuera is of stellar quality, although they diplomatically emphasize that it's just "different" from that in other villages. They wanted to capture this difference to share with those beyond the steep mountains that their village rests atop.

In 2003 they started with the main objective of making wines in La Figuera only from grapes within the village's boundaries. They named their winery Ficaria as it's the Latin name for the fig tree from which La Figuera takes its name as well. Little by little they've planting more vines to arrive at a total of 4ha that are almost all Grenache with a very small amount of Syrah and Cabernet Sauvignon. Some of their vineyards are up to 80 years old. Seven years ago they even planted some White Grenache to produce a white as the grape variety had disappeared from the village long ago.

They vinify the 8,000 bottles they produce each year mostly in stainless steel and clay tanks as Jaume wants to allow the true nature of the grapes to show as opposed to oak elements and cellar manipulation. To that end, he and Montse happily welcome guests to their winery so that they can directly experience where the wines come from and why they find them to be so special.

🟡 Matraketa 2013

A very limited production of just 280 bottles named after their youngest son. The nose is exquisite with notes of white pear, minerality, rosemary, and a touch of beeswax. Very elegant in the body and while full on the palate remains fresh and lively. The finish is quite even and lingers with green apple notes as well a little caramel.

100% White Grenache

13% | 12.50€

🔴 Èlia 2011

Named after their daughter, the nose holds mature dark fruits with a touch of plums. It's pleasing on the palate with a good structure. The finish is delicate with dark fruits the most prominent aspect.

70% Grenache, 20% Syrah, 10% Cab Sauvignon

15% | 13€

🔴 Pater 2010

Cured cherries in the nose along with currants, minerality, herbs, and a touch of light citric aromas. Smooth and round in the body, it presents a solid acidity that carries in to the lingering finish with notes of licorice and cherry pie.

100% Grenache

15.5% | 21€

🔴 Cerverola 2011

Aromas of chocolate, strawberries, and general red fruits with an all-encompassing freshness to it. The body continues with this theme of freshness as well as being elegant and smooth with a wonderful balance to it along with nicely defined acidity. The finish is light with just a touch of lingering acidity.

100% Grenache

15.5% | 35€

FICARIA VINS

Albert Coll
owner

GPS
41.1504227
0.8450123

Finca Fontanals

Falset, *Carretera N420, Falset-Reus, Km 844*

Visits: Call or email ahead for a reservation. The cost is 25€ for up to eight people.

Contact: 687465858, 637051662 | info@fincafontanals.com
Website: www.fincafontanals.com
Languages: English

At first the way you approach Finca Fontanals seems very curious as it involves driving down what seems to be a dirt road that says "don't enter" right off of a vista point on the main road to Falset. But, once you pass this inferred barrier you quickly come upon the small valley where the vineyards and cases rurals of Finca Fontanals call home. This land has been in Albert Coll's family for five or six generations and while they still have a home there, they also have two fully renovated homes for rent as well. One dates from 15th century and the other possibly even early.

One of the most curious features of this property is what at first appears to be little more than a small cave in to the side of the red rocks with a circular channel above it. Albert remembers playing around it as a child and thinking little of it until one day he dug out the cave, called up a historian, and found out that it's actually a very old wine cellar. How old? Well, based upon preliminary research it could be from 2,000 BCE as very similar constructions have been found over in the Caucus region. It was very simple in how it functioned in that they would put the grapes in the middle of the circle and crush them by feet. The juice would then drip in the 300 or so liter cave below which they would then seal and let set until wine emerged sometime later. While more forensic investigation would need to happen, it points winemaking being a very, very old activity in Priorat.

Surrounding this old winemaking spot is a lovely area with 8ha of vineyards that, while being DO Montsant, butts right up against the southern border of DOQ Priorat. It's from these vineyards with three different soil types on each side of the valley that they make their one namesake red wine. They have some white vines as well that they currently sell to other wineries, but hope to use for their own winemaking as well someday including their recuperation of the rare native white Vinyater grape. It's a great project with an exciting future ahead of it.

🔴 Finca Fontanals 2010

Red fruit notes of cranberry and raspberry as well as cloves and a touch of vanilla in the nose once it opens up. The body is balanced with a sandy texture to it that rolls in to a well-integrated finish with dark fruit notes and a pleasing, downplayed acidity that lingers.

40% Grenache, 30% Syrah, 20% Merlot, 10% Cab Sauvignon

13.5% | 16.90€

The old cellar cave

Andreu Bartolomé lays claim to having both the only cellar in the gorgeous historical village of Siurana, but also the highest altitude cellar in all of DO Montsant. He grew up in Barcelona but is from a family that originally lived in the village. He's the owner of Restaurant Siurana and he bought the land where the cellar sits to hold his wedding some years ago and started producing wines in 2007 from high altitude vineyards nearby. Totaling 2ha in size, they were originally family vineyards and sit at approximately 800m in elevation.

He has big plans for this small stone house and the cellar attached to it as he eventually wants to open up a small shop and bar in the warmer months to sell his wines as well as others from the region. Given that Siurana is a big attraction for visitors, it's bound to be a popular stop along the way as the views from it are nothing short of stunning.

Andreu Bartolomé
owner

GPS
41.260733
0.942007

Graus de Siurana

Siurana, *Carretera Cornudella-Siurana, Km 6.5*

Visits: Call ahead to arrange a tasting and visit.
Contact: 977821142, 686221085 | andreuimariasiurana@tinet.cat
Website: www.restaurantsiurana.com
Languages: English, French

● El Salt de la Reina 2005
Coffee and toasted bread notes along with mature red and dark fruits, pepper, and pineapple. Round in the body, it's very easy to drink with violet notes that carry in to the finish along with a dry aspect.
100% Grenache
13.5% | 7.80€

● Bertran de Castellet 2007
Aromas of raspberries, leather, and balsamic elements as well as floral notes of roses and violets. The body is smooth and round with a fresh acidity. For the finish there is a rather large explosion of red fruits that hang very nicely on the palate.
70% Grenache, 30% Carignan
13.5% | 14.50€

Roger Grifoll
co-owner & enolog

GPS
41.165193
0.705488

Grifoll Declara

El Molar, *Carrer de la Font, 7*

Visits: They offer visits for free depending on availability with prior reservation.
Contact: 977825149,626176474 | info@cgrifolldeclara.com
Website: cgrifolldeclara.com
Languages: English, German, Japanese

As with many cellars in the region, the Grifoll Declara family have been making wines for generations--seven that they know of in the village of El Molar since the early 1800's. They had to stop during the Spanish Civil War as this area was one of the frontlines during that brutal conflict. They were able to start again in the 1950s but it wasn't the commercial venture that it is today and was done primarily for family consumption and produced under their old family home.

That changed in the 1980s when they officially joined DO Tarragona and then moved in to their current cellar in 2001 which is a compact and efficient affair that sits at the east end of the village. They made this move just as DO Montsant was being formed. In the current generation of the family it's the son, Roger who oversees the wines after having formerly studied enology and worked for several years at Álvaro Palacios.

They produce wines both under DOQ Priorat and DO Montsant with the later accounting for the vast majority of their production, respectively 20,000 bottles and 150,000 in the two regions. Ironically, despite most of their vineyards being in DO Montsant, most of the family land is in the limits of DOQ Priorat (70% to be exact) but such is the dual nature of El Molar which sits split between both of the Denomination of Origins for the comarca.

Despite this large production, you'd be hard pressed to find the Grifoll Declara wines anywhere in Spain save but for a few local shops. They export 99% of their production out of Spain to 37 different countries with the USA being their main market.

🔴 El Gos 2013 ⚖️
Red fruits in the nose such as strawberries and raspberries with underlying notes of toast and touches of vanilla. The structure of the body is round overall with a good acidity and continued red fruit notes that carry in to the finish.

Grenache, Carignan, Syrah

14% | 7.50€

🔴 Tossals Junior 2012
An interesting mix of plums, cherries, licorice, cocoa, and leather to the nose. The body is medium in strength and departs from the nose a great deal leading in to a finish that shows barrel aspects in a manner that's a bit too pronounced.

Grenache, Carignan

14.5% | 10€

🔴 Tossals 2010
Red fruits, licorice, and cocoa aromas to the nose that are well balanced with one another. The body envelops the palate decently, but stays a bit short and closed overall while the finish is long with a mix of lingering red and dark fruits.

Grenache, Carignan, Cab Sauvignon

14.5% | 14€

🔴 Tossals Expressions 2010 ✴️
A delicate and complex set of aromas that focus on red and dark fruits, cinnamon, cloves, cocoa, orange peel and a touch of lactic notes. The body is quite full and ample with fresh acidity and round tannins that lead in to a lingering, elegant finish. A grand wine overall to be had with red meats or enjoyed by itself.

Grenache, Carignan, Cab Sauvignon

14.5% | 25€

GRIFOLL DECLARA

GPS
41.101184
0.751463

Celler Els Guiamets
Els Guiamets, *Carrer de la Esglesia, 1*

Visits: While not open for visits, their shop is open at the cellar Mon-Sat for wine purchases.
Contact: 977330055 | unió@unio.coop
Website: www.cellerelsguiamets.com
Languages: English, French, German, Italian

While out of sight, down on the side of Els Guiamets, the signs from the main road make it easy to find this old cellar that was built in 1913. And, for the past 100 years this cellar has been a pillar of wine production for the village residents and some from nearby areas as well. Like many, they started producing bulk wines from the grapes of the associates that joined the group, but have shifted to producing more bottles over the years, now laying claim to an output of 150,000 bottles, 90% of which are red wines.

The number of associates of the cooperative steadily rose after they started producing wine in 1916 to eventually peak at around 60. As time has gone on, the numbers have dropped with some choosing to produce and market their wines on their own or others just deciding to retire from the physically demanding work of vine cultivation. At last count they had about 42 active members of the cooperative who voted recently to sell the winery to Celler Unió to be able to face new market challenges while continuing to make their wines like they've always have. Unió is a group of over 20,000 farmers and a cooperative of cooperatives of sorts, which means that they help old cooperatives in the Tarragona province of Catalonia stay in business while keeping their peasant roots but changing their trajectories to be under the Unió umbrella.

From the summer of 2013, Unió has been running the cellar and marketing the wines, with Josep Anton Llaquet heading their enology. Whether or not they will change the lines of wines remains to be seen as they have a loyal following and they've managed to continually sell 60% of their very large production directly to their home market.

They also produce a very tasty DOP Siurana olive oil that they press in nearby Marçà.

🔴 Mas dels Mets 2012
Fresh fruits in the nose as well as touches of currants and other dark fruits. While the character is young, it's fresh overall with a finish that's a bit tannic.
Carignan, Grenache, Tempranillo
14.5% | 2.70€

🔴 Les Tallades 2010
Dark fruits, spices, and a touch of orange peel to the nose. The wine is light but with tannins too much in the background. It finishes with minor fruit notes.
Grenache, Cab Sauvignon, Merlot
14.5% | 5.90€

🔴 Gran Mets 2010 ★
Dark fruits, nutmeg, cloves, and smoky notes to the nose. The body is complex and meaty with strong but well controlled tannins. The finish brings the smoky notes back in to play.
Cab Sauvignon, Merlot, Tempranillo
14.5% | 9€

🔴 Isis 2006 ⚖
Notes of strawberries at the base of the nose along with toasted notes and balsamic elements. In the body it's round and agile leading in to a finish with licorice and menthol notes at the end.
Syrah, Grenache, Carignan, Cab Sauvignon
14% | 13€

Josep Anguera
co-owner & enolog

GPS
41.098362
0.702374

Joan d'Anguera
Darmós, *Carrer Major, 29*

Visits: There is a cost of 70€ for visits which are designed to be for a group of about 10 people. Call ahead for reservations.
Contact: 977418348,639270245 | josep@cellersjoandanguera.com
Website: www.cellersjoandanguera.com
Languages: English

The cellar of Joan d'Anguera is steeped in history. They've been producing wine in the same location ever since brothers, Josep and Joan's ancestor (from whom the winery takes its name) built the original house in 1820. To get to the original house you have to walk through a bit of what has become a rather large winery due to multiple expansions over the years that have allowed them to produce 100,000 bottles in a typical year.

They were one of the old family cellars in the regions producing bottled wines starting in 1984 when it was all still part of the DO Tarragona. Their vineyards are a mix of mostly Grenache, Carignan, and Syrah with small plots of oddball old grapes popping up here and there such as Puntxó Fort that some other wineries in Darmós have as well. In total they have 25ha of vineyards with the majority being between 35-50 years old.

Taking over from their father after he passed away at the turn of the century, Josep and Joan have been focused on continuing the family tradition. But, much like their contemporaries in DOQ Priorat they found that they wanted to make wines in a style more like the past while taking advantage of modern controls to ensure quality wines.

In 2009 they switched over to farming completely organically and biodynamically, receiving Demeter certification in 2012. They've traded the typical small oak barrels in the cellar for larger oak, used oak, and concrete tanks. Working to express what they consider to be the true essence of their vineyards, the first wine to be released with this new approach was the 2011 Altaroses.

🔴 Joan d'Anguera 2013
Aromas of dried apricot and plum. Slight undertones of hazelnuts and strawberries. Balanced and full in the body with good acidity that leads in to a dry finish. Overall typical elements of a young wine.

Syrah, Grenache

13.5% | 6€

🔴 Planella 2011
Aromas of black pepper, red fruits and a touch of chocolate. It's spicy in the body with a generally tannic aspect that carries in to the dry finish with notes of sage. Continually evolves as it breathes.

45% Carignan, 45% Syrah, 10% Grenache

14.5% | 10€

🔴 Altaroses 2011 ⚖️
Aromas of strawberry, thyme, subtle minerality, and a touch of balsamic elements. It presents a wonderfully pleasing body that's aromatic and flows in to a fresh, round finish with excellent red fruit notes. A truly excellent expression of the Grenache from the region.

100% Grenache

14% | 10-11€

🔴 Finca L'Argatà 2011 ★
Dark fruit aromas of plum and fig over an undercurrent of herbs. In the body it's very well-balanced with a round, smooth aspect. The fruit notes linger in to the finish slightly as it fades with touches of rosemary.

Syrah, Grenache

14.5% | 15€

JOAN D'ANGUERA

Noel Lang
manager

GPS
41.144653
0.809356

Laurona
Falset, *Camí de Falset-Bellmunt, Km 0.7*

Visits: Call or email ahead to schedule a visit and tasting at a cost of 12€ per person, up to 15 people maximum.
Contact: 977831712, 678710267 | laurona@cellerlaurona.com
Website: www.cellerlaurona.com
Languages: English, French

Just outside of the center of Falset on the road to the nearby village of Bellmunt, there sits a large modern winery which houses Laurona. It uses the Roman name for a single vineyard in the area which was noted to produce grapes of high quality by Pliny the Elder. The cellar was started in 1999 when René Barbier, the owner of Clos Mogador and Christopher Cannan, the owner of Clos Figueras (both of which are in neighboring DOQ Priorat) set out to create a winery in DO Montsant. They initially bottled the wines under DO Tarragona, Subzone Falset which, like the other wineries in this region, changed to DO Montsant in 2002.

Through its decade and a half of existence, René has continually proven that high quality, deeply profound wines can be produced from the villages of DO Montsant. All of their grapes come from about 10ha of vineyards located throughout the Priorat comarca including: Falset, Darmós, El Masroig, and of course the very well-known La Figuera which produces beautiful Grenache grapes that also find their way in to the L'Espectacle wine that is also produced in this cellar.

In 2009, there was a bit of a change and while René is still the enolog for the winery (along with Fernando Zamora), he and Christopher sold it to Josep María Mainat and Toni Cruz (who are popular Catalan comedians), along with Marcos Santana. They did a bit of rebranding, but have otherwise continued with producing great wines to the tune of 60,000 bottles a year.

Also of note is their organic olive oil that they produce under the Laurona name as well and, like the wines is absolutely delicious.

🟡 **Laurona Blanc 2012**
A blanc de noir with floral aromas mixed with tropical fruits such as mango. Citrus notes of grapefruit come in to play as it decants. Well defined in the body, it lingers on the palate for some time before fading out in a pleasing finish.
100% Grenache
13.5% | 14€

🔴 **Laurona Negre 2007**
Dark fruits in the nose with hints of graphite and notes of vanilla from the oak. It's round in the body and quite balanced overall with red fruits lingering in to the finish along with pleasant acidity. It could easily be aged for two years more if desired.
Cab Sauvignon, Carignan, Grenache, Merlot, Syrah
14.5% | 14€

🔴 **Plini de Laurona 2009**
Full of mature red fruits in the nose along with eucalyptus notes and a good deal of depth. The tannins in the body are very well structured presenting a round, elegant wine that remains quite fresh overall. A fine accompaniment for red meats as well as cured pork.
Grenache, Carignan, Syrah
15% | 22€

On the south side of Cornudella there is a small hill that pops up just behind the old art nouveau cooperative building. Here, sitting amongst the old village homes is the cellar of Malondro. It has a view over the village and despite initially appearing small in size, they are able to make 30,000 bottles a year here.

The cellar was started in 1999 when Joan Carles Estivill bought a small amount of vineyards in the village. This allowed him to produce a white and a red in 2001 under the name, Malondro. This is a curious name as it doesn't sound Catalan nor Spanish. Joan Carles explains that as far as they can ascertain, it was probably Italian in origin and is a name from his mother's family that he wanted to preserve.

The winery has naturally grown over the last decade and they now own 14ha of vineyards from which they produce their wines. Joan Carles is sure to emphasize that their wines are produced only from their own vineyards with Ramon Valls as their enolog. They currently export nearly 100% of what they produce outside Spain with just a few bottles to be found locally.

Joan Carles Estivill
owner

GPS
41.263784
0.905623

Malondro
Cornudella de Montsant, *Carrer de Miranda, 27*

Visits: N/A
Contact: 977821451,636595736 | jcestivill@malondro.es
Website: www.malondro.es

● **Negre 2011**
Balsamic aromas alongside dark fruits, touches of vanilla, and herbal sage notes. Plush and full in the mouth, it puts forth strong red fruit and pepper flavors that drift in a lingering finish with good acidity.
60% Grenache, 40% Carignan
14.5% | 15€

Jesús del Rio Mateu
Andreu Fernández
owner, enolog

GPS
41.146967
0.728578

Mas de l'Abundància

El Masroig, *Camí de El Masroig-Gratallops, Km 3*

Visits: Preferred on weekends. Call or email ahead to confirm.
Contact: 627471444 | info@masdelabundancia.com
Website: www.masdelabundancia.com
Languages: English

Jesús del Rio Mateu is a well-spoken man of letters and was a professor in Barcelona. Having published several books including those of his own poetry, he found himself at a crossroads in his life during his 40s while working in the Barcelona city government. He realized that his original home back in the village of El Masroig was calling him and he made the decision to buy a small property alongside the Siurana River and make the rest of his life there.

It's here that Mas de l'Abundància can be found today. His home is small and very comfortable set upon the property where the vineyards he planted nearly 20 years ago surround him today. This land was originally farmed by the Scala Dei monks back in the 15th century who might very well have known Jesús's family who have been making wine in the vicinity of the village for centuries only stopping with his father.

Now, in a good year, Jesús will see about 20,000 bottles emerge from his vines that climb up along the walls of the small canyon around this stretch of the Siurana, just outside the official bounds of what is now DOQ Priorat. His wines are produced almost completely from his own estate grapes with a few coming from a 100 year-old plot that borders his land.

Old vineyards

🟡 De Calpino 2012
Toasted aromas with mature apples, peach, gardenia, and a bit of dried flowers in the nose. The body is silky with a strong personality and a finish that rounds of the wine with the same qualities as the nose.
100% White Grenache
14.5% | 18.50€

🔴 He·Ma 2012
Fresh in the nose with red fruits, forest fruits and a touch of sweetness. A bit vegetal in the body, it also shows mature fruits and finishes well with good structure.
Cab Sauvignon, Grenache, Carignan
14% | 6-7€

🔴 Flvminis 2011
Dried red fruits such as raspberries and strawberries with a general floral quality. The body is balanced with good acidity. The finish is rather dry and a touch bitter at the end.
Cab Sauvignon, Carignan, Grenache
14% | 12€

🔴 Mas de l'Abundància 2012
Notes of dried figs with touches of menthol, leather, and incense. Quite full and structured in the body, it finishes with mature fruit and black olive notes.
50% Cab Sauvignon, 30% Carignan, 20% Grenache
14.5% | 20€

Joan Pujades Giné
owner & enolog

GPS
41.101802
0.750763

Mas de la Caçadora
Els Guiamets, *Avinguda de la Carretera, 9*

Visits: Call ahead to schedule a visit which are free with wine purchases.
Contact: 977413005, 656336877 | masdelacasadora@yahoo.es
Website: www.masdelacasadora.com
Languages: English

Meaning, "the house of the huntress", Mas del la Caçadora takes its name from a 6ha property that has 2ha of vineyards. From this small foundation, Joan Pujades Giné started up his winery with his first harvest in 2003. Little by little he has grown and now harvests from 12ha of vineyards spread over the villages of Els Guiamets, Marçà, Falset, and La Serra d'Almos. Ten are his own and two he leases from others.

He's able to produce 25-30,000 bottles a year in what he calls his "garage cellar". While this may conjure up an image of a space barely able to hold two parked cars, his cellar is actually quite large. It was originally a chicken farm located right in the middle of Els Guiamets on the main road. Joan has obviously retrofitted it a great deal for his wine production which gives the appearance of taking up every single bit of space to be found.

Amidst all the tanks and barrels, Joan makes use of a great variety of grapes such as Grenache, Carignan, White Grenache, Macabeu, Cabernet Sauvignon, Muscat, Merlot, and others to make his six wines.

One of their vineyards

🟡 **Tretze 2009**
White flower notes, but the nose is generally dominated by the aging regiment. The body is of medium strength and the finish is lingering but again has heavy aging notes.
100% White Grenache
14% | 13€

🟡 **Oreig 2009**
Floral aromas along with citric notes, honey, and jasmine. The body is a bit weak overall with a strong alcoholic component and the finish is heavily dominated by the potent Muscat characteristics.
White Grenache, Macabeu, Muscat
14% | 8.50€

🔴 **Limbeu 2009**
Aromas of pitted cherries and mature fruits. Large and round in the body, it makes for an agreeable wine with a dark fruit finish.
Merlot, Grenache
14.5% | 8.50€

🟠 **Panses**
Aromas of raisins, toffee, walnut and some orange peel in the nose. Very thick on the palate with a potent sweetness that is countered by citrus notes that continue in to the finish.
100% White Grenache
15% | 14€

MAS DE LA CAÇADORA

GPS
41.132197
0.824263

Mas d'en Canonge
Marçà, *Mas d'en Canonge*

Visits: Call or email ahead to schedule a visit and tasting at a price of 10€ per person.
Contact: 977054071,636974058 | celler@masdencanonge.com
Website: www.masdencanonge.com

When looking southward from Falset, the slim, modern structure of the Mas d'en Canonge winery doesn't seem too far off as it sits gleaming against the foot of the mountain, Llabería. Arriving there though proves to be something of a wine safari as both the lower and upper roads are old dirt trails just wide enough for a single car and feel as though countless generations of Priorat farmers have walked them. Of course once you reach the cellar, all of the plane unfurls out in front of you and on clear days it makes for a stunning view over a huge swath of the vineyards of DO Montsant.

The history of this cellar started back in 2000 when Salvador Alceda was looking to invest in a winery in the area. Having made his living in the hospitality industry, he saw the winery as a natural extension of his endeavors. He bought the Mas d'en Canonge property in 2006 and built the cellar right alongside the old masia from which the winery takes its name. In 2007 they made their first vintage under the expert guidance of local enolog, Toni Alcover who is an instructor at the enology school in Falset as well as the current president of DOQ Priorat.

The property came with a nice selection of vines ranging from 40-70 years old. To this they planted new vines that are now 8-10 years old and in total have about 7ha of their own vineyards to which they add the grapes from 6ha more that they buy. All told, they produce about 50-60,000 bottles a year, but as anyone who visits the cellar will note, they have the ability to produce even more in the future when they choose to.

🔴 **Sons Jove 2012**
Dark fruit and balsamic notes along with being a touch vegetal. A light, basic body, it ends with a dry, short finish.
Grenache, Carignan, Syrah
14.5% | 6€

🔴 **Ressons 2009**
A reduced quality to the aromas leads in to an initially smooth body with bitter notes that carry in to a dry finish that's a touch green.
Grenache, Syrah
14.5% | 12€

🔴 **Ressons Clot de la Vella 2009**
Fresh and vegetal in the nose leading in to a large and generally pleasing body and a lingering, dry finish.
Grenache, Syrah
14.5% | 18€

MAS D'EN CANONGE

In Catalan, "mas" is a short form of "masia" or old, country home. Thus, Mas Sersal would imply that there's a "Sersal" home somewhere to be found, but in reality the name is a portmanteau of the three winery owners: Gabriel "Mas", "Ser" from Sergi Montalà, and "Sal" from Salvi Moliner. Together they started this winery project in 2008 in a space in Falset that used to be the discotheque called, La Bauhaus. Salvi has worked as an enolog and Sergi is a somellier giving the two of them the skills to make the wines from the two properties in Falset, El Masroig, and Els Guiamet that they buy grapes from.

They've managed to create a popular series of wines that are well known with 90% of their 5,000 bottles being sold in Spain. But, it was the introduction of the "half-criança", Set Tota la Vida wine that has changed things. It's named after a 2007 album by the very popular Catalan band called, Mishima and the wine was released in 2013. While a band-cellar partnership may initially seem strange, it's all due to David Carabén, the band leader's childhood friendship with Salvi. According to Gabriel, it has sold very well and worked to further raise the profile of their winery.

Gabriel Mas
co-owner

GPS
41.144687
0.811118

Mas Sersal
Faslet, *Les Sort dels Capellans, 15*

Visits: N/A
Contact: 666415735 | vins@massersal.com, vins@estones.cat
Website: www.estones.cat
Languages: English, French

🔴 **Set Tota la Vida 2012**
Red and dark fruits in the nose with a character that's a touch lactic. The body is easygoing and round with good acidity that leads in to a light, slightly bitter finish.
Grenache, Carignan
14.5% | 11€

🔴 **Estones 2011**
A set of aromas comprised of dark plums, cocoa, and spices. The body has a good volume to it that maintains a pleasing balance between the fruit and acidity and is quite expressive, leading in to a deep, lingering finish.
Grenache, Carignan
14.5% | 17€

Josep Borràs
co-owner

GPS
41.234633
0.704007

Mas de les Vinyes
Cabacés, *Mas de les Vinyes*

Visits: Call or email ahead to make a visit to the cellar which are free. They can accommodate up to 12-15 people if visiting as a group.
Contact: 977719690,652568848 | josep@masdelesvinyes.com
Website: www.masdelesvinyes.com
Languages: English

There used to be a great many more vineyards in Cabacés but as time went on the people in this small village on the far west of the Priorat comarca grew more and more olives. The olives are indeed fantastic in this area and make delicious oil, but it feels like something was lost in this change as showed by how Mas de les Vinyes continues to make excellent wines from the region.

While offering a great deal of solitude, it's a lovely location with the vineyard of L'Espectacle just up on the top of the mountain next to them. Their masia, which is indeed in the middle of the vineyards, is from the 19th century and they have been growing vines alongside their olive and fruit trees for a very long time. They had been producing their own bulk wine, but with the start of DO Montsant, they restarted bottling their wines in 2000 and haven't looked back although they do still sell a little bulk wine.

Their oldest vines are Cabernet Sauvignon, Macabeu, Grenache, and Carignan. The Cabernet Sauvignon was planted as it was the style in the mid-20th century to plant French varietals, although unlike other locations the Cabernet does quite well in their microclimate. Little by little they've been planting more native Catalan grapes including White Grenache that they plan to add to their white wine down the road.

About 70% of their 35-40,000 they're able to sell without a problem right in Catalonia. The rest they export.

● **Blanc 2013**

Very light nose with touches of grapefruit, lemon peel, and lychee. Fruity and expressive in the mouth with citric elements and a clean, fresh finish with light acidity that lingers. A very different, lighter white from this region.

100% Macabeu

13% | 5.50€

● **Negre 2013**

Paprika, cumin and black pepper to the nose. The body is generally balanced with good acidity and red fruit notes that carry in to the finish. Develops some balsamic notes with time.

40% Grenache, 40% Carignan, 20% Merlot

15.5% | 6€

● **Criança 2010**

Elegant, light aromas of white pepper, red fruits, and herbs. Balanced in the body with chalk and clay textures that lead in to a clean finish with slight lingering bitter notes of lemon peel.

30% Cab Sauvignon, 25% Merlot, 25% Syrah, 20% Grenache

15% | 8€

● **Racó d'Atans 2010**

Red fruits and delicate herbal aromas to the nose. Fresh and light in the body, the red fruit notes come back in the finish which lingers with a light acidity and pepper notes.

60% Cabernet Sauvignon, 20% Grenache, 10% Merlot, 10% Syrah

15% | 10€

● **Racó d'Atans Selecció 2003**

Buttery balsamic notes in the notes along with dark fruits, dried figs, and allspice. Balanced on the palate but dry in texture. The finish is lingering, light, and elegant with some red fruit notes that fade out perfectly.

45% Cab Sauvignon, 25% Merlot, 15% Grenache, 15% Carignan

14.5% | 14€

MAS DE LES VINYES

Carles Escolar
enolog

GPS
41.126253
0.733642

Celler El Masroig
El Masroig, *Passeig de l'Arbre, 3*

Visits: Their wines, oils, and other local products are available at their shop which is open daily. They have scheduled visits on Saturdays and Sundays at noon for a cost of 8€ per person. For longer visits that include the vineyards at a cost of 10€, call or email ahead to reserve.
Contact: 977825026 | visites@cellermasroig.com
Website: www.cellermasroig.com
Languages: English, French

While the church may be the most visible building from the distance, the cellar complex of Celler El Masroig has to be the largest place in the entire village of El Masroig.

Just off to the side of the main road through the village, this cooperative cellar was, as stated above the main cellar, founded in 1917. Their facilities have at several times proved too small and they've built new cellars next to on another in order to take on additional production from what are now 500ha of vineyards spread amongst their 200+ cooperative associates. From this vast expanse of vineyards, they harvest 2.5 million kilograms of grapes annually.

These days they are far and away the largest producer in the region, producing literally millions of liters per year and exporting around the world. To put it in to perspective, they produce 60% of all the wine produced by the cooperatives and 30% of all the actual wine produced in DO Montsant. Despite how it was in the past where the cellars produced only bulk wines, Celler El Masroig produces an impressive range of 14 different bottles for all tastes ranging from basic bulk wines, to the very approachable young wines, to their aged and elegant criança bottles.

In recent years, they've worked to make their cellar accessible to visitors and offer regular tours that include visiting the old underground tanks that they've converted in to a barrel aging area and museum.

🔴 **Solà Fred Rosat 2012**

Great red fruit aromas to the nose composed of raspberry and a little cherry. Light, it also has herbal notes and leads in to a soulful body with a lingering acidity in the finish.

90% Grenache, 10% Syrah

13.5% | 5€

🟢 **Solà Fred Blanc 2013**

Peach, apricot, and white fruits in the nose. Fresh and crisp with good acidity that continues in to the light body presenting rather bold fruits and leading in to an equally strong finish that lingers with a touch of bitterness on the palate.

75% Macabeu, 25% White Grenache

12.5% | 5€

🟢 **Les Sorts Blanc 2011**

White fruit aromas in the nose with notes of peach and apricots skins as well as fresh notes of chamomile and toasted almonds. The body fills in the mouth, but stays light and leads in to a long finish.

100% White Grenache

13.5% | 10€

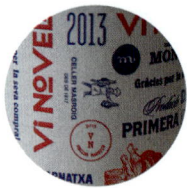

🔴 Vi Novell 2013

Red fruit notes in the nose along with a freshness that translates in to the body and makes for a wine that's very much alive in the mouth. A very versatile and approachable wine for immediate consumption.

Grenache, Carignan

13.5% | 6€

🔴 Solà Fred Negre 2012

Great presentation of dark fruit notes and a touch of licorice. Fresh and balanced in the body, it's a touch dry and leads in to a finish with short fruits notes. An excellent meal wine.

90% Carignan, 10% Grenache

14% | 5€

🔴 Les Sorts Jove 2013

Smoky plum notes from the maceration process. Full in the mouth and showing good dark fruits, the plum notes return in the finish and linger with a good dose of acidity.

40% Carignan, 30% Syrah, 20% Tempranillo, 10% Grenache

14% | 6€

🔴 Castell de les Pinyeres 2010

Spicy in the nose with red and dark fruits as well as blueberries and smoky notes. It has a very pleasing, velvety body and a finish that brings the aromas from the nose back in to play.

40% Carignan, 30% Grenache, 10% Merlot, 10% Cab Sauvignon, 10% Syrah

14.5% | 7.50€

🔴 **Les Sorts Sycar 2010**
Potent and intense with its long balsamic aromas. In the body it's ample and voluminous leading in to a dry, pleasing finish.
60% Syrah, 40% Carignan
14% | 10€

🔴 **Les Sorts Vinyes Velles 2008**
A clean, nose that's potent and full of forest floor and mature dark fruits. The body is ample and plush leading in to a lingering and very agreeable finish with sweet tannins.
35% Grenache, 50% Carignan, 15% Cab Sauvignon
14% | 14.50€

🔴 **Mas Roig 2007**
A blend of many aromas in the nose such as blackberries, black pepper, blueberries, rosemary, and earthiness. The body is light and a touch dry but balanced overall, leading in to a potent, but very controlled finish.
75% Carignan, 15% Grenache, 10% Cab Sauvignon
14.5% | 26€

Noguerals has wineries in both DO Montsant and DOQ Priorat. The Montsant project was started in 2000 utilizing a small, 1.5ha plot of family vineyards near Cornudella. These grapes were originally being sold to the local cooperative, but Ramon Alzamora found that they grapes were overproducing and he wanted to scale that back and focus on making as high a quality a wine as possible from them.

These original grapes are a mix of Grenache and Cabernet Sauvignon that are all at least 45 years old. In the last decade, they've also planted newer vines to have a grand total of 3ha that they harvest. This translates into 3,000 bottles a year released as the one Corbatera label. All of this is produced in their cellar in the center of Cornudella that originally used to be a bakery. They also conduct their tastings there which include the two wines from DOQ Priorat that are produced in the nearby Barranc de la Bruixa.

Ramon Alzamora
owner

GPS
41.265767
0.906407

Noguerals
Cornudella de Montsant, *Carrer de Tou, 5*

Visits: Call ahead to arrange a visit at a cost of 3€ a person to taste three of their wines. The fee is waived with purchases. Maximum of eight people.
Contact: 977821020, 650033546 | noguerals@hotmail.com
Website: www.noguerals.com
Languages: English

🔴 **Corbatera 2009**
Nutty aromas in the nose as well as good minerality, cloves, and bell pepper. The body is balanced and elegant overall leading in to a long finish with spices and notes of toasted almonds.
70% Grenache, 30% Cab Sauvignon
14.5% | 13-15€

Joan Asens
co-owner & enolog

GPS
41.163661
0.705152

Orto Vins

El Molar, *Cooperativa del Molar*

Visits: N/A
Contact: 629171246 | info@ortovins.com
Website: www.ortovins.com
Languages: French

Spend enough time in the wine circles of Catalonia and you will invariably hear the name, Joan Asens come up. He is known for being an incredibly top notch enolog in the region and because he was in charge of enology at the famous Álvaro Palacios winery in DOQ Priorat for some time. His intensity and devotion to winemaking can be a lot for casual wine drinkers to take in, but for anyone enamored about the process of winemaking and specifically nature-driven winemaking, he's a fascinating acolyte in the Church of Grape to talk to and in Catalan he is often called a "crac" which basically means a genius.

Joan believes in harvesting extremely late to allow the grapes to be at their maximum ripeness; an approach he says was how they actually used to harvest the grapes in the past. While he admits to losing some grapes to raisin, he is able to separate them during the harvest to make the Orto sweet wines. In addition to such quotes as "our factory is the sun", he's also a hardcore believer in using the lunar calendar not only for wine production, but also wine drinking.

Joan comes from a long family of winemakers who are from the village of El Masroig. Like many, his family had been selling their grapes to the cooperative for years once they stopped producing their homemade wines some 90 years ago. This all changed in 2008 for Joan, along with his cousin Josep Maria Jové and the brothers, Jordi and Josep Maria Beltran, who all owned old, classic vineyards around El Masroig. They decided to create a new winery together and funnel all of their grapes in to its production with Joan heading up the enology duties. Using the cellar of the old cooperative in El Molar, they created two lines of wines. Their regular line of wines are all from vineyards around El Masroig and are a mix of single varietal bottles and blends ranging from whites to reds to sweets which are all excellent.

It's the "Singularitats" that get most attention though as they're a series of only four monovarietal and single vineyard, limited bottlings. While one is a Carignan, the other three are grapes that aren't usually seen bottled singularly such as Tempranillo and Hairy Grenache. Then there's the Picapoll Negre which is a grape more common in DO Pla de Bages and hardly seen at all here.

These signature wines from Joan and his partners along with the regular line have garnered a great deal of praise and admiration as they set out to establish their wines as being a new style that's derived from old winemaking methods and old vines and respecting the cycles of nature.

🟡 Blanc Flor 2011
White fruits, anise, vanilla, and dried flowers in the nose. The body is elegant and seductive with an excellent texture in the mouth. The finish is long and delicate with notes of toasted almonds. A fine pairing for fish and white meats.
100% White Grenache
14% | 13.50€

🟡 Blanc Brisat 2011
Mature citrus aromas, dried flowers, and smokiness to the nose. The body is electric with a lively, marked acidity that carries in to the astringent but fresh finish.
100% White Grenache
14% | 15€

🔴 Orto 2011

Interesting aromas of blackberries and raspberries as well as herbal notes such as rosemary and a touch of lilac. The body is full with a cocoa character overall and a finish that carries this as well. An excellent all around wine that's easy to drink and pair with many dishes.

55% Carignan, 29 % Grenache, 6% Cab Sauvignon, 10% Tempranillo

14% | 10€

🔴 Les Comes d'Orto 2011

Fresh in the nose with light touches of brioche. Smooth and complex in the body it boasts lovely balsamic notes that come back in the light, pleasing finish.

50 % Grenache, 45% Carignan, 5% Tempranillo

14.1% | 18.50€

🔴 La Carrerada 2011

Smooth in the nose with mineral and cherry aromas. The body is very agreeable overall with a silky texture that leads in to a long, expressive finish. Could age for another year or two if desired.

100% Carignan

13.75% | 32€

🔴 Les Pujoles 2011

Aromas of baked apples and vanilla as well as a preserved cherries and mature figs. The body is medium strength and expresses well in to an elegant finish with a point of dryness at the very end. Could be well paired with grilled steak and a puree of chestnuts.

100% Tempranillo

14.15% | 32€

🔴 Palell 2010
Smoky with mature red fruits in the nose along with strawberries, cumin, and black pepper. Balanced in the body, it makes the palate salivate as it slides away in a lingering finish. Wonderful to have with bolder dishes or on its own.
100% Hairy Grenache
14.5% | 42€

🔴 Les Tallades de Cal Nicolau 2011
Red fruits in the nose intertwined with mature currants, licorice, pepper, wild strawberries, pomegranate, and lilac notes. The body is fluid and light, but with well defined, delight tannins. The finish is enveloping and expressive with light smoky notes at the very end.
100% Picapoll Negre
13.75% | 52€

🟠 Dolç d'Orto Blanc 2011
Starts with citric notes in the nose such as lime peel and orange blossoms that then shift to quince and dried apricots. The body is light, fresh, and subtle with touches of rosemary honey. Could be paired with countless dishes such as foie gras, blue cheese, cod, and others.
80% White Grenache, 20% Others
14.4% | 13.50€

🟠 Dolç d'Orto Negre 2010
Prunes, raisins, touches of orange, and caramel aromas. Fresh and light in the body, it shows slightly bitter notes as it ends in a finish with lingering balsamic aspects.
100% Grenache
13.6% | 13.50€

Toni Ripoll
co-owner & enolog

GPS
41.149054
0.829749

Pascona

Falset, *Finca Fontanals*

Visits: Call or email ahead to schedule a visit and tasting at a cost of 8€ a person and a maximum of eight people.
Contact: 609291770 | info@pascona.com
Website: www.pascona.com
Languages: English

Despite being so close to Falset, Pascona can be a bit hard to find. Turning at the road by where the local buses park and then veering to the right by a small chapel that sits in the middle of the road is a good start. Then, as you follow a northeast direction you'll come to the first of several signs that lead past what seem endless vineyards and eventually, the old family house with the cellar next to it.

There waiting to greet you will probably be Toni Ripoll, the son of the family who has taken over the winemaking and he may or may not be accompanied by lovable winery hound, Nord. The cellar is compact and full of tanks and barrels not only for Pascona, but also Comunica who make their wines there as well as the joint project of La Comèdia that Pep and Patri of Comunica commercialize.

All around the cellar stretch the vineyards which are 25ha in total with one part over 80 years old. It's a grand property and one that is from a family that has been prominent in Falset working as doctors and judges in the past. This history is from Toni's mother's side and the name of the property is derived from the name 'Pau' who was an ancestor of the modern family.

The vineyards sit on three different types of soil: clay, granite, and the special soil typical to DOQ Priorat which is llicorella. In fact, the dividing line between DO Montsant and DOQ Priorat is just 200m away from the Pascona vineyards.

Given that 25ha create a lot of grapes, Pascona sells off 80% of their production to other wineries in the area and with what they keep, they produce 50,000 bottles a year. From the mostly Grenache, Carignan grapes (with a smaller amount of Cabernet Sauvignon, Merlot, and Syrah) that they produce, they release eight different wines as Toni, like many others wants to try and express the locale as much as a possible in the wines that he creates.

🔴 **Trencaclosques 2012**
Red fruit aromas of strawberry and raspberry as well as notes of brioche. Full in the body, it finishes long with large fruits while maintaining its overall freshness.
100% Syrah
13% | 6-7€

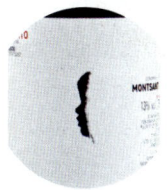

🔴 **Lo Petitó de Pascona 2013**
Mix of red and dark fruits with dried plum notes most prominent. Minor balsamic and spice aromas as well. Young and spicy in the mouth but still with a good deal of depth. Dry in the finish.
Merlot, Syrah
13% | 6-7€

🔴 **La Mare de Pascona 2012**
Dried figs, chalky minerality, and crushed red berries to the nose with an underlying hint of curry. Delicate in the mouth with notes of fresh black pepper which carry in to the finish along with lingering tart berries notes.
100% Grenache
13.5% | 19-20€

🔴 **Lo Pare de Pascona 2010**
Aromas of licorice, caramel, and old brandy in the nose. The body is pleasing and easygoing leading in to an astringent finish with notes of cherries.
Grenache, Cab Sauvignon
13.5% | 24-25€

Edouard Chevalier
enolog & manager

GPS
41.128207
0.803887

Portal del Montsant

Marçà, *Carrer de Dalt, 74*

Visits: N/A
Contact: 648922263,977178486 | info@portaldelmontsant.com
Website: www.portaldelmontsant.com

Originally this very large 101 year-old building was constructed for the cooperative of Marçà, but after merging Falset, it lay empty until Alfredo Arribas started the Portal del Montsant project in 2003. Initially working with enologs Ricard Rofes (now with Cellers de Scala Dei) and Eva Escudé (now with Trossos del Priorat) along with Edouard Chevalier who joined in 2008 they created a series of wines that garnered great acclaim for their unique character.

In 2010, Alfredo sold the project to the Penèdes winery Parxet and he started up a similar but new project simply called Alfredo Arribas in neighboring Falset. For the last four years, under Parxet's ownership the winery has continued in the same vein as the original concept with Edouard in charge of the enology.

The size and scope of Portal del Montsant is very impressive. For one thing there's the old 1913 building it resides in. Then there are the 150,000 bottles that they produce each year both for export and local sales. Strolling through the cellar is incredible as despite its size, it is packed full of tanks in all shapes and sizes. The reason for this is that they vinify every separate grape varietal and property separately. As they buy from a total of 35ha, this means they have tanks that are several thousand liters in size to just a few hundred. Below all of this there are the barrels that rest in what used to be the underground tanks of the cooperative.

Brunus Rosat 2012
A great deal of strawberry aromas in the nose. It is balanced overall in the body with a defined acidity that lingers quite long in the finish.
100% Grenache
13% | 10.50€

🟡 Bruberry Blanc 2012 ⚖

Notes of citrus, especially lemon peel alongside an undercurrent of tropical pineapple notes and white fruits. It has a rich, oily texture and good acidity with a floral finish.

100% White Grenache

13.5% | 10€

🟡 Santbru Blanc 2010

Notes of vanilla and white flowers along with a minor smoky aspect and dried fruits. It's big, round, and envelops the palate with a lingering quality that carries in to the finish with some minor notes of the barrel aging.

White Grenache, Grey Grenache

14% | 15€

🔴 Bruberry Negre 2011

A jammy nose with dark fruits. Very agreeable in the body and light while leading in to a relatively short, but still pleasing finish.

Grenache, Carignan, Syrah

14.5% | 10€

🔴 Brunus 2010

Aromas of chalk, red and dark fruits, as well as tobacco leaves and a touch of pink peppercorns. The body is full and elegant with freshness that opens very well with additional decanting. The balance of aging and expressing the natural fruits is excellent.

Carignan, Grenache, Syrah

14.5% | 13€

🔴 Santbru Negre 2009 ⚖

Aromas of prunes and blueberries along with spices such as black pepper, cloves, and cumin. The body is wondrously elegant, round, and plush with a perfect balance of acidity and tannins. This leads in to a persistent finish with the spice elements lingering on the palate.

Carignan, Grenache, Syrah

14.5% | 18€

Joanne Cox
co-owner

GPS
41.260753
0.90672

Ronadelles
Cornudella de Montsant, *Carretera Cornudella-Porrera, Km 0.6*

Visits: In combination with their restaurant they offer countless tasting options like a full wine and food tasting menu or vineyard visits in an actual London taxi. Call or email to schedule a tasting to your needs and group size.
Contact: 977821104 | ronadellessl@hotmail.com
Website: www.ronadelles.com
Languages: English

The roots of Ronadelles started when Jaume Giral met Englishwoman, Joanne Cox in Tarragona. After working intense schedules in their respective jobs that often conflicted with seeing one another, they realized that they wanted a change of pace in their lives. Moving to Jaume's birth village of Cornudella in Priorat they started their restaurant, La Serra in what used to be a sawmill. Shortly after, in 2002 they started up the cellar named after a trail that runs from their property up to the Siurana Reservoir.

Jaume's family had vineyards for years which they were able to immediately use for their wines and allowed them their first vintage in 2003. As their production grew they started leasing others vineyards from local growers in the village. The majority of the vines are Grenache and Carignan with a bit of Macabeu and Syrah as well.

For some time, the cellar maintained itself at a regular level of production and up until just four years ago they were making 18,000 bottles a year. Their most recent vintage saw a jump to 100,000. Many attribute this marked increase to their "Cap de Ruc" label which means "donkey head" in Catalan. With the donkey being the national symbol of Catalonia and the independence movement gaining a great deal of momentum in recent years, it's easy to assume that people are buying the wines purely out of patriotism. Joanne counters that while that might be some of it, the main reason is due to consistently creating a good, affordable wine with solid distribution which is easy to see in the wine range of bottles that they offer.

🔴 **Petit Rosat 2012**
Initially, aromatic notes of currants. Light on the palate it boasts good acidity and a slightly voluminous quality that ends in a short finish full of red fruit notes.
Grenache, Syrah
14% | 5.50€

🟡 **Cap de Ruc Blanc 2012**
Herbaceous and mineral in the nose with menthol notes along with a touch of volatility. Very intense in the body, but well-balanced with freshness and aging. The finish lingers without being heavy and giving citric notes.
White Grenache, Macabeu
13.5% | 4.50€

🟡 **Petit Chardonnay 2012**
Mineral in the nose with white floral notes and pineapple that carry in to a fresh body with notes of white pepper, ending in an easygoing, quick finish.
100% Chardonnay
13.5% | 6€

RONADELLES

🟡 **Petit Blanc 2011**
Complex notes of pine, golden apples, fresh bread, and magnolia that flow in to an unctuous, throaty body and ending with a long finish that's just a touch bitter.
White Grenache, Macabeu
14% | 7€

🔴 **Cap de Ruc Garnatxa 2012**
Strong notes of acidity in the nose as well as touches of carob. The body is light overall and very direct with an astringent finish.
100% Grenache
14.5% | 4.50€

🔴 **Petit Negre 2010**
Mature dark fruits in the nose along with notes of blackberry and violets. The body is very agreeable on the palate and finishes with mature fruits and a good structure.
Grenache, Carignan
14.5% | 9€

🔴 **Cap de Ruc Criança 2010**
Notes of allspice, resin, and chocolate. Slightly sweet in the body, it's general fresh and finishes quickly and dryly.
Grenache, Carignan
14.5% | 7.50€

🔴 **Giral Vinyes Velles 2006**
Aromas of currants, raisins, vanilla, and fig. The body is fresh and intensely mineral with a touch of cedar and balsamic notes, ending in a long and complex finish.
Grenache, Carignan
14.5% | 15€

🟠 **Cap de Ruc Dolç**
A wonderful bouquet of aromas in the nose including dried figs and cherries. Round in the body, it's wonderfully sweet, but lacking in acidity for balance. The finish is very long.
Grey Grenache
15% | 9€

Their London taxi out in the vineyards

Albert Peris started out with an 85 year-old plot of Carignan vines that his grandfather had planted. A small plot of just 1,500 vines on 0.5ha of land, he worked a great deal to recuperate it and began to bottle the Sant Antoni in 2008 as a tribute to these family vines.

Never a big production, the Sant Antoni ranges from 200-600 bottles each year which are made via natural fermentation at the cellar of Venus La Universal. As time has gone on, he's been joined by Jordi, Xavi, and Helios who also make the garage wine Ratpenat together.

Albert Peris
co-owner & enolog

Sant Antoni
Falset

Visits: N/A
Contact: albertperis@msn.com

● **Sant Antoni 2011**
Exotic spice notes of cinnamon and cloves in the nose along with a slight bit of mossy minerality. The body is balanced, full, and fresh with good acidity that perks up a bit more in to the finish that has notes of dried plum and fig.
100% Carignan
14% | 15€

Pilar Just
Xavier Peñas
owners

GPS
41.135848
0.854806

Sant Rafel
Pradell de la Teixeta, *Ctra. La Torre-Pradell, Km 1.7*

Visits: Available and free with prior reservation via email or phone.
Leave the Car: They are located just 300m from the Pradell de la Teixeta train station.
Contact: 689792305, 659484666 | info@solpost.com
Website: www.solpost.com
Languages: English

The Sant Rafel winery has the distinction of being the only cellar in the small village of Pradell de la Teixeta. It's a curious, wild location off by itself and it's this aspect that attracted Xavier Peñas and his wife, Pilar Just to the location 17 years ago. Both Xavier and Pilar were originally from Priorat, but like many they left to live in Barcelona for some time. After having enough city life, in 1997 they decided to move back and found this 46ha property and became enchanted with it.

With the sharp mountain of La Mola looming over their property to the east and a fresh breeze blowing up their the small valley that holds Sant Rafel, it's easy to see why they chose to make their home there amidst one of the most scenic vineyard locations in all of DO Montsant.

It's an atypical location as the house isn't actually that old and was built at the start of the 20th century whereas most of the masies in this region date back several hundred years or more. The family who lived there were growing nuts and produced a small amount of white wine at home. Xavier and Pilar decided to expand upon this and planted vineyards on the property immediately after buying it. Once they started having their first harvests, they sold them to the cooperative in Falset. In 2003 they started making their own wines and have just been growing ever since to now produce about 40-45,000 bottles a year.

It's also important to note that their Solpost Blanc 2011 was selected by a tasting panel to represent what DO Montsant white wine "is" at fairs, professional tastings and other promotional events.

🟡 **Solpost Blanc 2011**
Toasted aromas along with vanilla and mineral notes. The body shows mature fruits that carry in to an intense finish with white flower notes.
100% White Grenache
14% | 11€

🔴 **Joana 2012**
Generally red fruit notes in the nose as well as caramel and fresh acidity. The body stays light and fresh with a dry and slightly bitter finish.
Grenache, Carignan
14% | 6.50€

🔴 **Joana Selecció 2009**
Rather tight in the nose with red fruits and minor mineral notes. The body is full of very mature fruits that lead in to an astringent, short finish.
100% Grenache
14% | 8.50€

🔴 **Solpost Fresc 2009**
Toffee notes over a foundation of buttery aspects to in the aromas. The body is light and generally acidic with an astringent finish.
80% Grenache, 10% Cab Sauvignon, 10% Merlot
14% | 9€

🔴 **Solpost 2007**
Graphite minerality in the nose as well a touch of cocoa, currants, and vanilla. The body is fully structured and direct. The finish leaves a pleasing touch of dark fruits on the palate.
Grenache, Carignan, Cab Sauvignon
14.5% | 15€

SANT RAFEL

Josep Serra is originally from the bordering comarca of Ribera d'Ebre where he was a third generation winemaker, although with the past generations of his family, their wines were just for the local market. He studied enology and worked for the Falset-Marçà cooperative until 2002. He then worked for Mas Perinet until 2009 at which point he started up his own enology consultancy that now takes him all over Spain.

In 1998 Josep had purchased just over 2.2ha of vineyards in Capçanes that were planted in 1940 and during these years of working for other cellars, he was selling the grapes to other wineries in the area. In 2009 he moved to his own cellar and started to produce his one wine, Octonia in the village of Els Guiamets.

Of the 5,000 bottles he produces annually, about 85% are exported.

Josep Serra
enolog & owner

GPS
41.102378
0.751544

Serra i Barceló
Els Guiamets, *Carrer de Sant Lluís, 12*

Visits: N/A
Contact: 649670430 | josep@serra-barcelo.com
Website: www.serra-barcelo.com

🔴 **Octonia 2009**
Rich nose of dark, velvety fruits as well as downplayed hints of wild spices. Rich and buttery on the palate there are also mineral notes that become more apparent with air. Slight floral accents appear as well that complement the well-structured tannins. With more time it gets a bit unruly and wild.
50% Grenache, 35% Hairy Grenache, 15% Carignan
15% | 35-40€

Ulldemolins is the northernmost village in the Priorat comarca and it's here that, Santi Vinyes (whose last name means 'vineyards' in Catalan) has the most northern vineyards. Planted on terraces of red llicorella soil at an altitude of over 750m, he began harvesting them and making his own wine in his garage cellar in the village, in 2007.

Coming from a family tradition of winemaking, they had long been members of the local cooperative as well as home winemakers and wanted to do something more personal with these vineyards that he feels are quite special. Planted 15 years ago and now totaling 4ha, the view out from the vines is indeed striking, looking at the north face of the Serra del Montsant mountain on the other side of the valley.

Santi is able to produce about 4-5,000 bottles a year in three different labels and he also grows olives. Of the wines, he exports a little to the US and China, but sells most of it at home.

Santi Vinyes
owner

GPS
41.323711
0.877036

Serra Major
Ulldemolins, *Carrer de Alfons I El Cast*

Visits: Call ahead to arrange a visit which are free and offer a chance to taste the wines and visit the vineyards.
Contact: 647986960 | santi@sarroges.com
Languages: English (with prior notice)

● Teix 2010
Mature plums which verge on being a touch ferric. The body is round and easy to drink leading in to a light, but slightly bitter finish with notes of red fruits.
Grenache, Cab Sauvignon, Syrah
13.7% | 6€

● Gran Sarroges 2009
Aromatically full of mature plums, and preserved cherries, as well as gingerbread and crème of cassis. The body is highly tannic though which carries in to the finish with an overtly alcoholic aspect to it.
Grenache, Syrah, Cab Sauvignon, Merlot
14.9% | 14€

Siuralta is a wine from vineyards at an elevation of 750m that are at least 60 years old and growing on chalk soil near the small, stunning, cliff dwelling village of Siurana, thus the Siurana+Alta name (alta means high.) It is part of an upcoming "Vins Nus" or "naked wines" project which has a goal of really showcasing the fruit, locale, and truly wonderful nature of these grapes.

As something of an experimental and unique wine by Alfredo Arribas made in his Falset cellar, they don't make it every year and do date only the 2008 and 2012 vintages exist.

Alfredo Arribas
owner

GPS
41.144681
0.810976

Siuralta
Falset, *Les Sort dels Capellans, 5*

Visits: N/A
Contact: 932531760 | alfredoarribas@portaldelpriorat.com
Languages: English, French, Italian

● **Siuralta 2012**
Fresh and expressive in the nose. Aromas of leather, cloves, graphite minerality, and black pepper. Balanced and extremely pleasant in the mouth with a light, elegant finish that lingers forever.
100% Carignan
13% | 28-35€

Antoni Sánchez-Ortiz comes from a highly technical background. After receiving diplomas in different types of chemistry and working in a technical capacity in the corporate world, he took a course in wine tasting which then turned his life in a completely different direction. He studied enology at the Universities of Tarragona and Bordeaux and for the last decade has been an enologist at various wineries around Catalonia and overseas. His partner in the Saurí project is David Barriche who likewise comes from a technical background, specifically working in the field of wastewater management until he too changed paths to start earn a degree in agricultural engineering and enology.

Saurí is their project in DO Montsant started in 2010. Meaning "water diviner" in Catalan, it's a reference to the fact that grapevines in the region search long and deep in the ground to find water in the poor soil. The wine is made organically and with natural fermentation, as they work to create a wine that is as direct an expression of the region as possible.

David Barriche
Antoni Sánchez-Ortiz
owners & enologs

GPS
41.143352
0.817236

El Solà d'Ares

Falset, *Passatge Cèsar Martinell, 4 2n 4rt*

Visits: Call or email ahead to make an appointment. Visits are 10€ and take about 2-3 hours, including a walk around the vineyards.
Contact: 606995952 | info@soladares.es
Website: soladares.es
Languages: English, French, German

🔴 **Saurí 2011**
Dark fruit aromas in the nose mixed with a touch of licorice, spices, and black pepper. The body is fresh, light, and a touch dry with a finish that's also a little dry and somewhat short.
Grenache, Carignan
14.5% | 12€

Ruud Persoon
owner

GPS
41.140164
0.706209

Terra Personas
El Masroig, *Carretera El Masroig-El Molar, Km 3.4*

Visits: Offered on a limited basis with scheduling ahead and with a maximum of eight people. The cost is 4€ per person, but is waived with wine purchases.
Contact: 662214291 | ruud@terrapersonas.com
Website: www.terrapersonas.com
Languages: English, Dutch, German

When heading from El Masroig to El Molar, you pass one of the old bridges typical of the Priorat comarca that cross the Siurana River. Almost immediately after this bridge, there's a small dirt road on the left that's easy to miss, but is the beginning of the road leading to Terras Personas. Driving along this you start making your way up the hill that forms one side of the small valley that the Siurana snakes through. There at the top, amidst a mix of vineyards and olive trees, you come the old home that Ruud Persoon has taken up residence in since 2006.

While to an English speaker his name sounds like "rude person", he's anything but and happily welcomes people to his vineyards. Originally from Holland, he set out to create a winery in this region in 2005 after being something of a hobbyist and lover of wine for years in his native country. It took until 2009 to buy all the properties that now comprise his 10ha of land that have 4ha of vineyards and the same in olive trees which are all dry farmed.

He has a mix of newer and older vines with Carignan that dates back 40 years and which he finds to be the best grape among all of them. By buying grapes to produce his white wine, he has slowly grown over the last few years and now produces 25,000 bottles annually using cellar facilities at El Masroig.

It's definitely a solitary place to call home, but it's easy to appreciate the tranquility it affords Ruud when looking out from his home across the valley and out to the Ebre River in the distance.

🟡 Blanca 2012
White flowers in the nose along with green fruits and some light herbal notes. The body is wonderfully intense and well-structured leading in to a persistent, defined finish with spices and herbal notes.
55% Macabeu, 45% White Grenache
12.5% | 7.50€

🔴 Vermella 2012
Forest fruits and tobacco as well as herbal notes of thyme and rosemary in the nose. The body expresses the fruit elements very well and finishes with lovely fat fruit notes.
45% Carignan, 40% Grenache, 15% Syrah
14% | 7.50€

🔴 Negra 2010
Intense with dark fruits, pepper, cocoa, and herbs such as rosemary in the nose. Round and voluminous in the body it has some slightly jammy notes before leading in to a fresh, elegant finish that lingers wonderfully.
80% Carignan, 10% Grenache, 10% Syrah
14.5% | 11.50€

Josep Maria Vendrell
co-owner & enolog

GPS
41.122425
0.813913

Vendrell Rived

Marçà, *Carretera Marçà-La Torre Fontaubella, Km. 1.7*

Visits: N/A
Contact: 637537383 | jmvendrell1@gmail.com
Website: www.vendrellrived.com

Josep Maria Vendrell is a young winemaker who sits at the helm of a family winery that, like countless others in the region goes back generations upon generations. As was typical up until just a few years ago, they were selling off all of the production from their 12ha of vineyards to the local cooperative. They then built their own cellar in 2000, initially releasing the wines under DO Tarragona and switching to DO Montsant just two years later when the region was officially established.

The winery and the vineyards, which are spread over six properties, sit at the base of the striking mountains that the Marçà village rests against. Here, Josep Maria is producing about 20,000 bottles in a good year and making use of a great many old vines that were planted by his grandfather. Looking to the future, he hopes to have full organic certification for his vineyards in 2014.

Moreover, Josep Maria produces a very interesting natural wine called, Wiss. He makes a small production, so it can be hard to find beyond a couple of shops in Barcelona specializing in natural wines.

A vineyard cat attacks his nemesis

🔴 **Seré 2012**

Tosses out a burst of aromatic intensity that focuses on forest fruits along with pepper notes. The body backs off a bit and is more restrained and light leading in to a finish that's persistent in the mouth with the forest fruit elements coming back at the end.

Grenache, Carignan

14% | 7€

🔴 **Miloca 2012**

Notes of blackberries, blueberries and black pepper in the nose. The body is a touch dry while remaining light, fresh and with a pronounced acidity that leads in to a decidedly dry finish with red fruit notes.

100% Grenache

14.6% | 8€

🔴 **L'Alleu 2011**

From their selected old vines, it shows mature red fruits in the nose. The body is overall light, balanced, and fresh, leading in to a dry finish with bitter notes that carry mineral aspects of the soil.

60% Grenache, 40% Carignan

14.5% | 12€

VENDRELL RIVED

René Barbier IV
Sara Pérez
owners, enologs

GPS
41.1548
0.820962

Venus La Universal

Falset, *Carretera de Falset-Porrera, Km 1*

Visits: N/A
Contact: 977830545,639121244 | info@venuslauniversal.com
Website: venuslauniversal.com

Clos Mogador and Mas Martinet are well known amongst lovers of the wines from DOQ Priorat. The names of their respective owners, René Barbier (IV) and Sara Pérez are also just as well known for both the incredible wines they craft as well as the fact they married years ago and started a new, grand wine family of Priorat. While they both have taken over their family wineries with great success, they wanted to start a new project to call their own and so in 1999, Venus La Universal was born.

The goal was simple: to produce high quality wines in DO Montsant. They buy all of their grapes from local growers and absolutely everything is certified organic. René handles all the cellar work while Sara handles all the viticulture. They built the cellar right next to their house within the borders of Falset and it was designed to be a personal project. Vinification and aging are done in more neutral receptacles such as concrete, clay amphorae, very used (up to 10 year-old) barrels from their Mogador and Martinet wineries, and very large, old barrels of several hundred liters that they've imported from different cellars in Europe.

The name of the cellar was originally just to be called, "La Universal" and have a tongue in cheek theme harking back to the grand titles of the early 20th century which you can see in the label designs. Venus came about as they wanted to incorporate the Greco-Roman names for a variety of reasons including the region's history and a return to a more natural, straightforward wine. This is the name they give to their stellar top end bottle, but the two younger red and white wines are named, Dido. These were originally to be called, Eneas as he was the son of Venus. It made for a logical continuation of their theme, although the name unfortunately conflicted with a wine already called, Eneas in Rioja and thus they settled upon Dido with whom Eneas had fallen in love.

During this cellar's 15 years of existence, the wines have proven to be very popular and they sell the majority of their 100,000 bottles directly to the Spanish market with the city of Barcelona alone consuming 30% of them. As it can be hard to find these wines outside of Catalonia, people who love Sara and René's ability to create such wonderful wines in any project they're a part of might just need to make a trip to the region to fully appreciate them.

● **Dido Blanc 2012**
Notes of citrus and lemon peel along with apricot, jasmine flowers, and brioche. The body is wonderfully balanced and full, leading in to a long and charming finish that picks up some of the citric notes of the nose.
Macabeu, White Grenache
14% | 14.50€

● **Dido Negre 2011**
Intense aromas focused on red fruits with touches of licorice. The body is light and immediately approachable with a long finish that holds buttery fruits and spices.
75% Grenache, 15% Syrah, 5% Merlot, 5% Cab Sauvignon
14% | 13.50€

● **Venus 2008**
Wondrous aromas of dark fruits such as blackberry and blueberry in the nose along with notes of licorice, tobacco, and cocoa. The body is profound with a vibrant freshness and the notes of the aging coming forth to make a strong, round wine that drifts off in to a lingering, elegant finish.
Carignan, Syrah, Grenache
14% | 28€

Joan Salvador
co-owner

GPS
41.127078
0.801487

Vermunver
Marçà, *Carrer de Ricard Pique, 15*

Visits: Contact them to make an appointment. The cost for a visit and taste is 5€ but is waived with a purchase. They also have a casa rural for rent.
Contact: 977178288, 686143240 | info@genesi.cat
Website: www.genesi.cat
Languages: English, French

The story of the Vermunver cellar is like many in DO Monsant in that they've been making wine longer than anyone in Joan Salvador's family can really remember. As most growers in the region have done throughout the 20th century, they had been selling their grapes to the local cooperative. But, starting in 2004, they began keeping some of them to produce a limited amount of their own wines to the tune of 18,000 a year. Prior to 2008, they exported mostly to the US, but since then have shifted to selling mainly in Catalonia and Central Europe.

Along what seems to be the main street of Marçà sits their family cellar. From the outside it's nearly nondescript with just a large old door marking its location in what is a rather typical, sign-less fashion. The inside is a compact affair set about in this first floor of this 18th century building with various tanks and barrels taking their positions. Joan says that it may not be fancy but it fully meets their needs which upon tasting their excellent wines is more the obvious.

It's Joan's son, Roger who heads up the enology duties and makes all the wines with natural fermentation while also following the biodynamic calendar which is the gospel to many of the winemakers in DO Montsant. The Vermunver wines that they produce are quite unique in that they are only made from single grape varietals.

One of their old vineyards

🔴 Vinum Domi 2012
Dry herbs and forest fruits to the nose with a body that is fresh and light overall. The finish is astringent and dry, but with notes of red fruits.
Grenache, Carignan, Merlot
13.5% | 5.50€

🔴 Petit Gènesi 2011
Red fruits with touches of cherry, balsamic, and black pepper in the nose. The body is fresh and a touch dry, but light in the mouth. Overall the finish serves to bring back the notes from the nose.
Grenache, Carignan, Syrah
14% | 7.50€

🔴 Gènesi Selecció 2008
Forest fruits as well as floral notes of lilac and violet to the nose. The body is full and fills in the mouth with well-balanced tannins that are a little dry. The finish is also dry, but gives the sense of a grand, aged wine.
Grenache, Carignan
14.5% | 13.50€

🔴 Varietal 2011

Lovely dark fruits aromas, subtle touches of licorice and earthy moss. The body is round with very fine tannins present that lead in to a lightly acidic finish with notes from the nose. An excellent wine for larger meals or to enjoy on its own.
100% Carignan
14.5% | 18€

VERMUNVER

While in plain sight, the winery for Viñas del Montsant is easy to miss. Just off the road to the west of Falset and behind a horse corral, there sits a large, anonymous building with green and white stripes that houses the winery. There is no sign and they're not open for visits, but while this is the modern incarnation of the winery, it's actually been in existence since 1919 and is currently owned by the Penedès giant, Freixenet.

They make their wines from various small plots around DO Montsant. Their flagship, the Fra Guerau takes its name from a 12th century friar of some renown named, Guerau Miquel who was responsible for building two hermitages in the region.

Judit Llop
enolog & manager

GPS
41.1401221
0.7982443

Viñas del Montsant

Marçà, *Carretera N420 Falset-Móra la Nova, Km 2.2*

Visits: N/A
Contact: 977831309 | fraguerau@fraguerau.com
Website: www.fraguerau.com

Garbó Rosat 2012
Dried strawberries, cola, and smoky aromas to the nose. Notes of bread in the body as well as red fruits and rose petals. Fresh and clean in the finish.

70% Grenache, 30% Syrah

13.5% | 6€

Fra Guerau 2010
Crisp red fruits to the nose along with white pepper notes. Full and balanced in the mouth, it has a kick of spice as well as dryness that carries in to the lingering finish.

Merlot, Grenache, Syrah, Cab Sauvignon

14.5% | 9€

Joan Ignasi Domènech
co-owner

GPS
41.081751
0.806108

Vinyes Domènech

Capçanes, *Camí de Mas Collet, Km 3.5*

Visits: Contact them to make an appointment. The cost for a visit and taste is 15€.
Contact: 670375828, 607192820 | jidomenech@vinyes-domenech.com
Website: www.vinyesdomenech.com
Languages: English

You set out in a southerly direction from Capçanes to find the cellar of Vinyes Domènech. While located far up in the hills and requiring the crossing of several points that warn of the potential flooding, the road is well marked by the signs of the currently closed, Hotel La Heredad Mas Collet. Three kilometers in, you start climbing in elevation quite fast, following this old, single lane road that seems to lead to little more than vineyards. But slowly an amphitheater of mountains closes around you and you inevitably see what led family founder, Joan Ignasi Domènech to plant his vines here a couple of decades ago.

Growing up a Falset native, he would scamper about these hills in the name of youthful exploration. As he grew older and started a family, he decided to purchase about 17ha of land in this area that already had some 50-60 year-old vineyards to which he added a great deal more. He now cultivates 9.5ha of vineyards across six different properties including 3ha of the generally elusive Hairy Grenache grape. All of the vineyards are certified organic these days and in addition to the Grenache grapes, they also grow a little Syrah, Cabernet Sauvignon, and Merlot. It needs to be noted that they are in an extremely unique microclimate which sees them harvesting the Grenache at the end of October when most other cellars harvest at least a month earlier.

The modern cellar where they make all their wines now is rather recent, having been built in 2009. Given that they are quite far from Capçanes proper, they've done what is possible to make the structure as green as possible with solar panels and built-in air circulation to reduce the need for using the generator. Their efforts didn't go unnoticed and they've won an award for cellar sustainability while producing about 55,000 bottles a year.

All of which Joan Ignasi happily shares at length with anyone who visits his cellar.

🟡 Rita 2012
White fruit notes of pear and peach as well as floral notes of rose and jasmine. It has a rich and full body that finishes long and profound on the mouth with lingering touches of honey and fruit.
100% White Grenache
14.5% | 15-16€

🔴 Bancal del Bosc 2012
Large aromas of dark fruits and herbs such as thyme and fresh rosemary. The body is light with mineral, chalky qualities. The finish is long and elegant in the mouth.
Grenache, Cab Sauvignon, Syrah
14.5% | 9€

🔴 Furvus 2010
Aromas of dark fruits and mature cherries. The body is wonderfully fat and round in the mouth yet stays fresh and balanced. Balsamic notes linger lightly in the finish.
Grenache, Merlot
14.5% | 15-16€

🔴 Teixar 2010
Amazing in the nose with its aromas of forest fruits, ginger, thyme, fennel, as well as cloves and hazelnuts. Fresh and elegant in the body it is also ample and balanced with round tannins that lead to a lingering finish with notes of fruit and oak.
100% Hairy Grenache
14.5% | 34€

VINYES DOMÈNECH

Just across the road from Darmós proper sits the modern cellar of Vinyes d'en Gabriel that was built in 2001. This of course is just the current manifestation of a winemaking family that dates back over 150 years. The ancestor of current owner, Josep Maria Anguera was Joan Rofes. He worked to build up and maintain the vineyards with a vision of them passing on to future generations. All of the wines were made in their old family home in the center of Darmós and it continued this way until the 21st century.

Josep Maria wanted to continue this vision of his ancestors but he realized that he needed a larger and more modernized cellar, so he made the decision to construct one in the middle of what have been the historical vineyards of his family. Josep Maria is able to work with a good amount of Grenache and Carignan vines that are at least 70 years old and some even up to 100.

He's planted new vines as well to add to the old and in total has 15ha of vineyards in Darmós and 7ha in La Figuera from which he produces his 40-50,000 bottles of a wine each year.

Josep Maria Anguera
enolog & owner

GPS
41.099878
0.704084

Vinyes d'en Gabriel
Darmós, *Carretera a Darmós*

Visits: While not available during the harvest, visitors are welcome the rest of the year at a cost of 10€ per person for a visit of the cellar, vineyards, and a taste of the wines.
Contact: 977418307, 609989345 | info@vinyesdengabriel.com
Website: www.vinyesdengabriel.com
Languages: French

🔴 L'Heravi 2013
Red fruit notes and cherries in the nose along with slightly vegetal aspects. Fresh and clean in the body with a little pepper and good acidity that leads in to a quick finish with minor acidic notes and tart cranberry.
60% Grenache, 20% Carignan, 20% Syrah
13.5% | 5€

🔴 L'Heravi Selecció 2012
Herbal notes with a tinge of balsamic elements in the nose. Light and balanced in the mouth with a defined acidity floating over red fruits. The finish is dry and lingering with the red fruit, leather, and licorice notes.
50% Carignan, 50% Syrah
14.5% | 7€

Garage Cellers

The following wines are all made in vinification spaces and from grapes within the region of DO Montsant. These are **not** however DO Montsant wines as they have neither cellar nor bottle certification. They are wines made by winemakers in the region as experiments or personal projects and have very small productions.

Despite this, they provide an interesting window in to what winemakers do in their spare time and what might possibly turn in to some of the region's newest, official wines.

Coma is born from a vineyard that has been in Cesc Parellada's mother's family for some time. Planted some 60 years ago by his grandfather, Cesc had been working these 2ha of vineyards with the family and selling the grapes to the Capçanes cooperative. Planted on a soil that's unique to the area and like red sandstone, most all of this small vineyard is Grenache with a very small amount of Carignan at the bottom of it.

In 2007 Cesc made a bold move to stop selling to the cooperative and start making his own wines. With the help of fellow villagers and friends, Antoni Bonfill for the viticulture and Jordi Barceló for the enology, little by little they've been creating vintages of their namesake Coma (which means a "valley amongst the mountains", not the medical condition) as well as the young wine Entre Cometes which means, "quote, unquote". To date these have been made outside DO certification and featured label design by various artist friends including Marina Capdevila and Andreu Zaragoza.

Antoni Bonfill
Cesc Parellada
Jordi Barceló
owners

Coma
Capçanes, *Carrer Major, 1*

Visits: N/A
Contact: 667912283
Languages: English, Portuguese
Website: www.coma.cat

🔴 Entre Cometes 2013
Fresh, clean red fruits and white pepper in the nose and is a touch vegetal. Fresh and light in the mouth it expresses its youth, but works to be a friendly wine to pair with meals.
100% Grenache
14.3% | 4.50€

🔴 Coma 2011
A bit wild in the nose with rustic aromas as well as a touch of toffee and blueberries. While not large on the palate, it has a solid central acidity that carries in to a long finish with cocoa aspect.
75% Grenache, 25% Carignan
14.7% | 9.50€

Pau Margalef was originally part of the Coma wine gang, but in 2012, he started making his own wines with a couple of his friends. They're all Capçanes locals and he merely refers to them as Ramon and "the twins", Josep and Marc. They all contribute their grapes from various small vineyards just in the village of Capçanes to make Trossos. While all are classic local varietals of Grenache and Carignan the vines range from 15-20 years up to some that decades old. La Padri is again a contribution from everyone, but mostly comes from a very young vineyard owned by the twins.

All told they only make about 500 bottles of each wine and each year they try something a little bit different.

Pau Margalef
co-owner & enolog

Pau & Amics
Capçanes

Visits: N/A
Contact: N/A

🔴 **La Padri 2012**
Initially there are aromas of sweet apples and mint. The body carries this to some extent and is in general sweet although with slightly more acidity developing and carrying in to the finish.
90% White Grenache, 10% Macabeu
14% | 3€

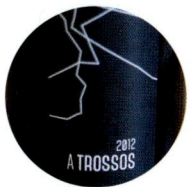

🔴 **Trossos 2012**
Herbaceous notes of basil and thyme are in the nose. Red fruits develop in the body with a velvety texture that leads in to a finish which is slightly sweet.
60% Grenache, 40% Carignan
15.5% | 4€

In 2011, the same group of friends who make the Sant Antoni wine together (Helios Carrasco, Albert Peris, Jordi Puxeu, and Xavi Chavero pictured above from left to right in front of portraits by Marina Capdevila) started making Ratpenat. The name in Catalan means "bat" which is the reason for the label created by Marina that shows the four of them upside down.

It's a curious wine as it's made with full natural fermentation and no oak aging whatsoever. The grapes that go in to it they purchase from other local growers, but the production is small with a total of 1,000 produced each year.

Albert Peris
co-owner & enolog

Ratpenat
Falset

Visits: N/A
Contact: albertperis@msn.com

🔴 **Ratpenat 2010**
An initially wet, barnyard nose with clay and mango aromas along with some minor red fruit and lactic touches. Generally even tempered in the body, the red fruits are stronger with a little minerality again backed by the lactic elements that lead in to a short, dry finish.
60% Grenache, 40% Syrah
14.5% | 8€

Notes

Redo Anguera
Page 131
Clonic